THE
STORY OF
CARPETS

I would like above all to thank my father for fostering in me the love of carpets. He was also my first teacher on the subject and to him I still defer. My special thanks also to Victoria Barclay who encouraged me to embark upon this book seven years ago and who has helped tirelessly with good advice and ideas. Jodie Jones, too, has given many hours of hard work for which I am enormously grateful. Finally, I reserve a great big thank you to all my clients and friends who make both being in the business of carpets and the love of them such a joy, and to all those who contributed their carpets to this book.

Any enquiries concerning the carpets illustrated in this book should be made to the address given below, quoting the reference number of the carpet.

Essie Carpets
62 Piccadilly
London W1V 9HL
Tel. 071 493 7766
Fax. 071 495 3456
or contact
P.O. Box 2242
London NW8 7SF

Published by Studio Editions Ltd
Princess House, 50 Eastcastle Street,
London W1N 7AP, England

ISBN 1 85170 727 1

Printed and bound in Singapore

THE STORY OF CARPETS

ESSIE SAKHAI

STUDIO EDITIONS

LONDON

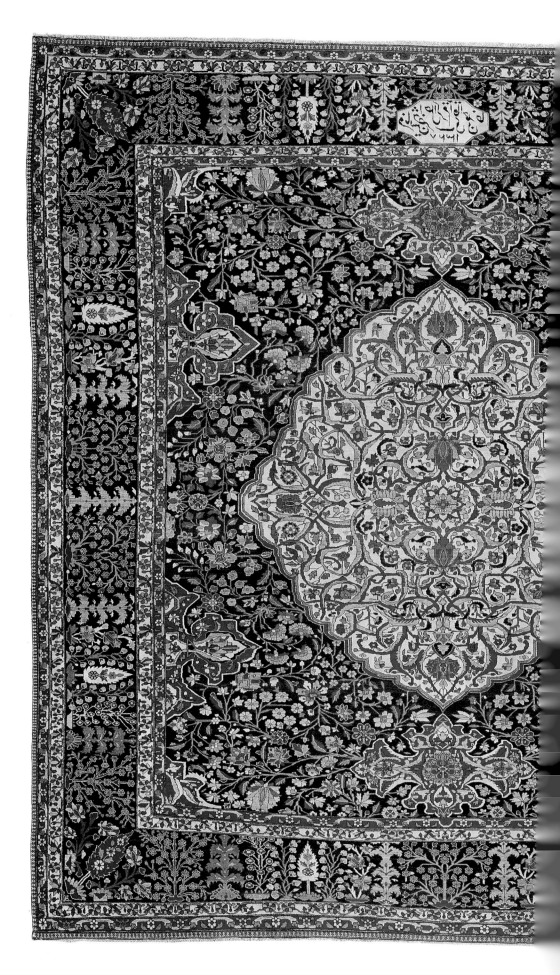

Half-title page –

Medallion within a plain field, Doroksh, wool on cotton, late nineteenth century, 21'0" × 17'0" (Ref. 1580)

Typical in design although not in size, this is another example of Doroksh weaving in which a simple triangular medallion and corners, filled with ornate multi-coloured floral filagree, are laid on a plain ground to great dramatic effect, with a beautifully integrated multiple border.

Bakhtiari medallion design, Chahar Mahall, wool on cotton, dated 1327 AH (1908/9 AD), Inscribed: *Farmayesh Hazrat Akram Agha Ahmad Khan 1327* ('Made to the Order of the most noble Ahmad Khan 1908/1909 AD') 15'8" × 14'7" (Ref. 359)

An elaborate carpet of unusual design and fine workmanship. Ahmad Khan does not appear to have been one of the Great Khàns of the Duraki, the ruling family of the Bakhtiari, and he may be identifiable as Ahmad Charshortori. The fine weaving and unusual design of this carpet make it a rare example.

CONTENTS

IN THE BEGINNING

IN A FAR AWAY LAND

UNRAVELLING THE TALE

READING THE PICTURES

SETTING THE SCENE

THE SEARCH FOR TRUTH

UNTOLD RICHES

DIRECTORY

CONTENTS

IN THE BEGINNING

IN A FAR AWAY LAND

UNRAVELLING THE TALE

READING THE PICTURES

SETTING THE SCENE

THE SEARCH FOR TRUTH

UNTOLD RICHES

DIRECTORY

CHAPTER ONE

IN THE BEGINNING

When you buy an oriental carpet, you are not just choosing an object of great beauty to enhance your home, you are buying part of a great tradition which stretches back to before recorded time.

Academics have argued long and hard over precisely where and when the first carpets (or, more accurately, simple floor coverings) were made. Some favour the early Egyptians, others the Chinese or even the Mayas. Others argue that all these people and more probably began to make carpets at about the same time. Though they had no contact with each other, they were driven by the same impulse to make themselves warm and comfortable. Woven carpets were softer than animal skins, and therefore more suited to their purpose. At this stage carpets were unlikely to have had any artistic pretensions, they were simply functional items.

It was only as the life of these early peoples became easier that they were left with the time to ornament themselves and their surroundings. We know that this began many centuries before Christ – the many cave paintings which still remain around the world indicate that early man very quickly began to explore his artistic talents. It is likely that the earliest carpet designs were similar to these cave paintings, depicting stylized scenes of hunting, animals and people.

Opposite –
Ziegler, Arak (Sultanabad), north-west Persia, wool on cotton, late nineteenth century, 24'1" × 18'4" (Ref. 1631)
The firm of Zeigler & Co., of Swiss origin and based in Manchester, England, was one of the largest exporters of printed textiles to Turkey and Iran in the second half of the nineteenth century. It began to import Persian carpets to England and then in 1876 set up its own factory at Arak (then Sultanabad) in north-west Iran. It remained in production until the firm closed in 1934 and much is known about its history and products. Given their enormous popularity as furnishings in wealthy homes throughout Ziegler's active life as a manufacturer and importer, it is not surprising that very many have been badly worn or destroyed. The present carpet is a splendid example of Ziegler weaving at its best, although the green used for the vast open field is quite rarely found and is a very splendid feature. During the last ten years, Ziegler carpets have once again become very popular in Western homes.

Tekke ensi, central Asia, wool on wool, second half of the nineteenth century, 4'11" × 3'11" (Ref. 1555)
This weaving is an *ensi* by the Tekke Turkoman tribe. *Ensis* were used as coverings for the tent entrance and were previously known to Western writers by the name *hatchli* after their cross-pattern. Despite their apparent resemblance to prayer rugs, there is no evidence that they were ever used as such. The design and colour of this piece is typical of Tekke weaving in the late nineteenth century and it is a very handsome example of this famous type.

Some of the earliest literary references to carpets are made in the Old Testament and in many classical writings, including Homer's *Iliad* and the plays of Aeschylus. In *Agamemnon*, Clytemnestra strews fine carpets at the feet of her home-coming husband. He protests that to walk on these carpets is an honour reserved for the gods, though eventually he is persuaded, much against his will:

Great the extravagance, and great the shame I feel
to spoil such treasure and such silver's worth of webs.

It is apparent, even from this brief example, that by the time Aeschylus was writing, in about 500 BC, richly worked carpets were being made, and were held in high esteem.

In fact, the earliest surviving carpet dates from about the same time. It is called the Pazyryk, after the region in the Altai Mountains of Siberia where it was found. This beautiful carpet, piled in wool on a wool and camel-hair foundation, formed part of the funerary accoutrements of a Scythian prince. In ancient times, the bodies of the wealthy and aristocratic were buried with all the possessions necessary to ensure their passage to the next life and the preservation of their earthly status there. Such tombs made rich pickings for grave robbers and the Scythian prince's tomb was robbed shortly after it was sealed. The carpet, however, was left behind and ironically this robbery ensured its preservation, since the imperfectly sealed tomb allowed water to seep in which then froze into

The Lion, Gabbeh, south-west Persia, wool on wool, twentieth century, 6'8" × 4'1" (Ref. 1535)
This is a charming example of a well-known group of Gabbehs called 'lion rugs' which have been made famous through a large, well-documented and widely travelled exhibition of such pieces organized by a noted Iranian sculptor and writer on tribal weaving. The lion has always had great symbolic significance in Persian history, both before and after the Arab Conquest when Islam was introduced. It is, of course, especially associated with the Imam Ali and is thus of particular significance for Shi'a Muslims. This piece, with its scattered flower, bird and animal motifs, is almost certainly by the Qashqa'i of Fars.

perma-ice, protecting the rug from ageing and decay. It remained untouched until 1947, when it was discovered by a Soviet archaeological team.

It is clear from the great skill with which this carpet was made that the practice of weaving must already have been well established before this time. Although the Pazyryk carpet is the earliest complete carpet in existence, there are fragments from earlier times which have been attributed to many parts of the Near and Middle East. Since these carpets were mostly made of wool, many thousands more must simply have decayed over the centuries. Recently, findings of complete pile weavings made entirely of flax have been published. These textiles, which are probably bed-covers, were excavated in the Tomb of Ka in Egypt earlier this century and have been preserved almost undamaged. They date from about 1,500 BC, some 1,000 years before the Pazyryk.

There are a variety of carpets and fragments, both piled and flat-woven, which date from between the fifth and fifteenth centuries AD. Many are associated with the Coptic Christian culture of Egypt and Nubia and are generally dated to between the sixth and ninth centuries. The earliest Turkish rugs are usually dated to the Seljuk period between the twelfth and fourteenth centuries and there are also many Spanish rugs from the fourteenth and early fifteenth centuries made by the Moors and therefore part of the Islamic weaving tradition. Nothing much survives of complete or nearly complete Persian carpets from before the early Safavid period at the beginning of the sixteenth century.

Medallion Islemi, Esfahan, wool on silk, twentieth century, signed: Iran–Esfahan–Mamouri, 7'8" × 5'1" (Ref. 650) After Sirafian, Mamouri was the best-known and most highly regarded Esfahani *ustad* (master-weaver) of the late Pahlavi period (1925–1979). This rug exhibits a design often associated with him, an undulating 'split-palmette' arabesque surrounding a central medallion, the arabesque being known in modern weaving circles by the Farsi word *islemi*.

Gol-bol boul, Tabriz, silk on silk, twentieth century, signed: Azim Zadeghe Tagie Zadeh, 9'10" × 6'7" (Ref. 1614)
It is interesting to compare this extremely fine woven rug with the Sirafian rug from Esfahan with the *gol bolboul* design, also very finely woven and whose beautiful colouring and quality make it very rare

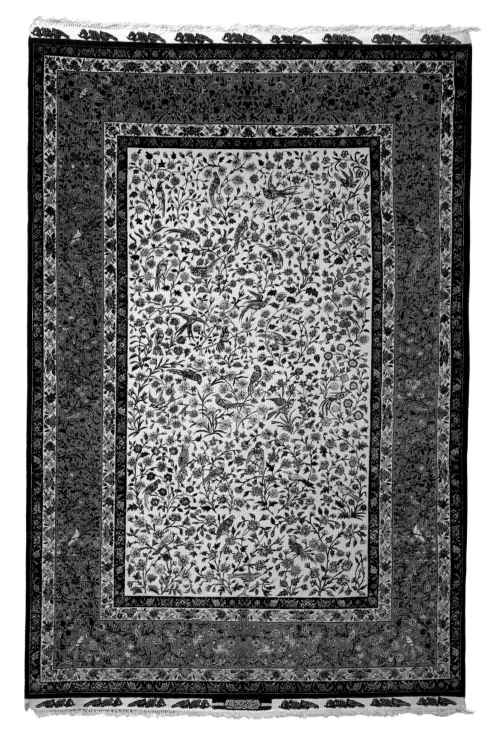

The 'Ardebil' carpet, now in the Victoria & Albert Museum in London, is probably the best known of all old Persian carpets. It is one of a pair which came to England in 1893, virtually in tatters. The decision was made to sacrifice one carpet so that the other could be restored. The cost of this work was prohibitively high, even for a museum, and it was only after an extensive public appeal that sufficient funds were raised for work to go ahead. There can be little doubt that in this case the end justified the means. The carpet, measuring 38' long by 18' wide, is an extremely fine specimen bearing an inscription by the weaver. This inscription reads:

> I have no refuge in the world other than thy
> threshold. There is no protection for my head
> other than this door.
> The work of the slave of the threshold
> Maqsud of Kashan in the year 946.

Translating this date into the Christian calendar shows that the carpet was woven around the years 1539–40 during the reign of Shah Tahmasp, one of the great patrons of carpet weaving. The incomplete remains of the other 'Ardebil' carpet, which bears the same inscription and date, was given by J. Paul Getty to the Los Angeles County Museum.

Other great carpets exist now only in legend. Of these, perhaps the most famous is the Spring Carpet of Chosroes. Chosroes I was a Persian king who ruled from 531–579 AD. To celebrate his defeat of

'Ardebil' carpet (By courtesy of the Board of Trustees of the Victoria & Albert Museum)

Medallion within a plain field, Doroksh, wool on cotton, late nineteenth century, 15'5" × 13'9" (Ref. 1581)
Another large, squarish carpet from Doroksh and one which is again rendered memorable by the simplicity of the field motifs and the large expanse of plain royal blue field piled in remarkably lustrous wool. These are among the most dramatic of late Qajar and early Pahlavi period weavings.

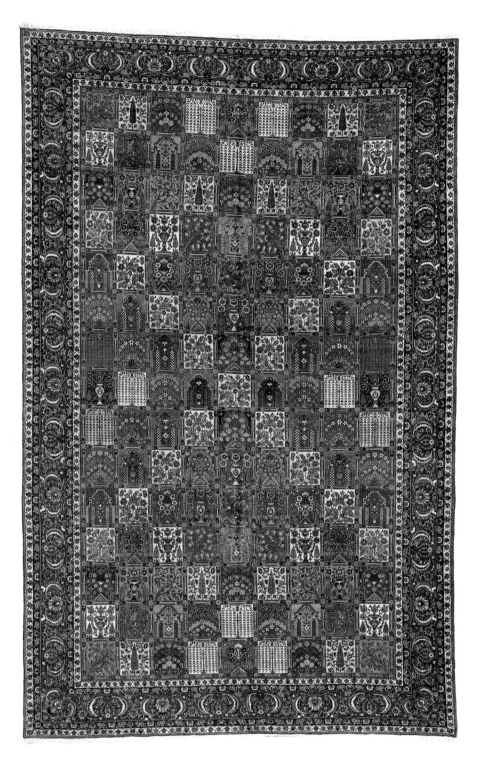

Bakhtiari design, Chahar Mahall, wool on cotton, mid-twentieth century, 19'10" × 12'8" (Ref. 1088)
Another splendid example of the 'garden-tile' design associated in particular with the Bakhtiari-owned factories of the Chahar Mahall Valley west of the city of Esfahan. Within the beautifully coloured panels are miniature *mihrabs* (prayer arches), *gol farangi* ('foreign flower'), roses, cypresses, some of which flank ornate vases, and in some instances – most noticeably on the white ground panels – chevron-like patterns which are stylized versions of the *bid majnun* ('weeping willow').

Opposite –
Bakhtiari garden design, Chahar Mahall, wool on cotton, early twentieth century, 19'9" × 14'9" (Ref. 1568)
One of the most famous of the late nineteenth – early twentieth-century designs, now usually called the 'garden tile' pattern. It is obviously a descendant of seventeenth-century garden carpets which, in highly stylized versions, continued to be made by Kurdish weavers throughout the eighteenth and nineteenth centuries, ending in the almost complete geometricization seen here. During the last 120 years such rugs, although produced in many different regions, have become especially associated with the Chahar Mahall workshops owned by the Bakhtiari *khans*. This is a very good example with exceptional colour; note the *gol farangi* pattern in the main border.

the Romans and his conquest of southern Arabia he ordered that a wonderful carpet be made. It was very large, perhaps as big as 400' long by 100' wide, and represented a garden; it was inset with hundreds of jewels. In such an arid country, gardens were highly prized, and this carpet was so large that the king could walk around its 'paths' and admire the fruits and flowers worked in precious stones and gold thread. Unfortunately for present-day enthusiasts, the Sasanian Persians were defeated by Arab invaders at the Battle of Ctesiphon in 641 AD and the Spring Carpet, which was one of the great treasures of the Royal Palace of Ctesiphon, was cut into pieces as booty.

By the advent of Islam in the seventh century, carpet weaving had already been in existence as an art for at least 2,000 years. However, from this time on the history of Islam became in many ways the history of the carpet. As the faith was spread by warlike tribes, a large part of the Near East and Central Asia was converted and subjugated, and this effective centralization of power created a stable society. The energies which had once been put into war were

Toodeshek Medallion (pair), Nain, wool on cotton, first quarter of the twentieth century, 7'0" × 4'7" (Ref. 1542)
In contrast to some of the other Nain carpets illustrated in this book, which use colours typical of post-war weavings from this city, this example, with its dominant reds and blues, has a closer affinity with early twentieth-century Sarouk and Kashan rugs. Even in recent times little attempt has been made to document Persian carpet making, but it is generally accepted that weaving began in Nain before World War II; this rug is an example of this quite rare early type.

now directed towards artistic and social achievements.

A brilliant period of Islamic art began with the rise to power of the Seljuks, a Turkic people from Central Asia, in the twelfth to thirteenth centuries. As the Islamic artistic style flourished under court patronage, the great artists began to apply the same designs to carpets. In Persia, existing geometric patterns were gradually replaced with more refined, flowing patterns. Particularly popular was the range of designs based on the central medallion which was also a firm favourite of illuminators of the Koran, the Islamic holy book.

Weaving was not limited to carpets. The nomadic people, living in a largely barren and arid land had, and still have, a

Medallion, Kashan, wool on cotton, first half of the twentieth century, 12'6" × 8'10" (Ref. 1333)
A very elegant and quite typical example of Kashan weaving, which is usually of very high quality. The elegant border pattern on a dark blue ground is also quite characteristic. It is unusual for its quality and size.

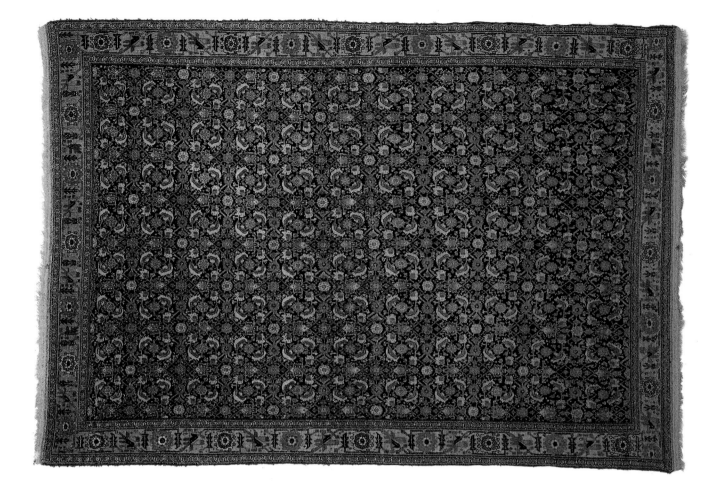

All over herati design, Senneh, wool on cotton, early twentieth century, 6'2" × 4'3" (Ref. 1612)

Senneh, a Kurdish enclave in north-west Persia, has been renowned for its weavings since at least the end of the eighteenth century, both piled and flat-woven. Fine Senneh *kilims* are among the most highly valued of all nineteenth-century Persian weavings and seem to have been greatly admired by the Qajar Shahs. This pile rug has lovely colour – note in particular the yellow ground borders – and an elegant rendering of the *herati* pattern in the field.

consuming passion for colour and pattern. Thus every household item, from the great bags which were their 'cupboards' to the bridles of their horses and camels (the nomads' most prized possessions) were fashioned from intricately knotted or woven pieces. But carpets were not just prized for their beauty. For both city dwellers and nomads they were also a symbol of financial security. While some carpets were necessary for a comfortable life, others were woven for sale in the bazaars, or kept as a sort of insurance in case of financial hardship later on.

The trade in carpets probably reached Europe for the first time with the return of the eleventh-century crusaders. Certainly by the fourteenth century they were so popular that they began to appear in European paintings. Italian artists frequently used these richly patterned rugs in their works and many great public figures, including Queen Elizabeth I of England, were painted against a background of carpets. Indeed, one type of richly patterned red carpet is still sometimes known as 'Holbein', after the court artist in whose paintings they so often appeared. Another is called 'Lotto' after the sixteenth-century Italian painter for the same reason.

At this time styles were constantly being refined and developed, often under the patronage of the court. No one dynasty had more influence on carpet production than that of the Safavids, who ruled through the sixteenth and seventeenth centuries. It was during this period that court painters were first given the opportunity to influence designs, resulting in some of the finest carpets ever made. At the same time carpets reached new heights of popularity in Europe.

In fact, these intricately worked – and expensive – carpets were so popular in France that the flood of money out of the country began to affect the economy. King Henry IV of France was so disturbed by this that he ordered that carpet workshops be set up within the French borders to counteract the trend. One of those weavers commissioned by the king was a certain Lourdet, who was established under royal patronage at the Hospice de la Savonnerie, in Chaillot, which was once a hospital. The carpets produced in this workshop borrowed much from oriental traditions, but also incorporated elements of the rococo style which was so fashionable at the time. The rugs were dubbed 'Savonnerie', after the building in which they were produced, and the name came to be applied to all

Jean de Dinteville and George de Selve, "The Ambassadors", by Hans Holbein (The National Gallery, London)

European, wool on cotton, mid-twentieth century, 17'9" × 14'1" (Ref. 797)

Throughout the late nineteenth and twentieth centuries, factories in many European centres have produced luxurious carpets in many styles but often, as here, inspired by the French products of the Savonnerie and Aubusson factories in which delicately arranged floral motifs predominate. The palette of many of these rugs is also similar, with an overall play on shades of beige, deeper brown and pink with the subtle pastel effects seen here.

Mughal miniature of Shah Jahan, mid-seventeenth century (India Office Library)

French rugs made in this distinctive style.

Henry was so impressed with the beauty of these rugs that he decreed that only the royal family could purchase them – thus rather defeating his original object of cutting down on oriental imports. With time some Savonnerie rugs found their way back to the East, and some oriental weavers, equally impressed with the design, began to produce their own versions. For once, taking coals to Newcastle proved to be a worthwhile endeavour!

Though carpets fell from popularity in eighteenth-century Europe with the advent of neo-classical design, they continued to be produced in great numbers. Trade was brisk between the great carpet centres of the East, and the carpet factories, or workshops, flourished. By the end of the century, however, carpets staged a comeback in Europe. The Victorians were great travellers and had a passion for all things oriental. The rich colours and intricate patterns of Eastern carpets were perfectly suited to their tastes.

Once again, Europe influenced the work of the weavers, as carpets incorporating family coats of arms and national symbols were commissioned. Royal families from as far afield as Portugal and Poland spent vast amounts of money on enormous pieces designed especially for their palaces and country homes. One Polish nobleman, Prince Czartoryski, lent a number of his seventeenth-century Persian silk rugs to the Exposition Universelle in Paris in 1866. Because of their ownership, one French critic in writing about the rugs assumed them to be of Polish manufacture and called them 'Polonaise'. Although this error was soon recognized and their Persian origin acknowledged, the name stuck for the whole group of these splendid seventeenth-century Esfahan silk rugs. One of the wonderful Czartoryski 'Polonaise' rugs is now in the Metropolitan Museum, New York.

As all things oriental became increasingly fashionable, the

Medallion, Sarouk, wool on cotton, early twentieth century, 6'9" × 4'1" (Ref. 632) Sarouk rugs of this unusual design are known in the trade as 'Mohajeran'. Certainly this bears little resemblance to what one normally thinks of as Sarouk design, as can be seen from a comparison with a number of characteristic examples in this book. One cannot help but admire the brilliant control of design and colour in this piece, the former being particularly complex.

carpet workshops found themselves hard-pushed to meet demand. As production speeded up, so quality began to suffer, with hastily woven rugs sold in bulk to an uninformed public. The Persian weaving industry entered a period of creative decline.

Perhaps the most notorious development was the introduction of aniline dyes, discovered in 1856 by an Englishman, Sir William Henry Perkin, while trying to synthesize quinine. Initially these dyes, probably the most famous of which is a purple called fuchsine, were quite expensive and although they came to be used in oriental carpets from about the 1870s onwards, they were not used in large amounts, but simply as bright highlights here and there. As more and cheaper dyes were synthesized and marketed, however, they were used in ever-increasing amounts, although their use in Persia does not seem to have been as extensive in the late nineteenth and early twentieth centuries as it was in Turkey. It was soon realized, however, that they were very light-fugitive and either changed colour or became dull and muddy, spoiling the appearance of a rug. Various attempts were made to outlaw their use, with the Persian government threatening dire penalties, including mutilation, for anyone found using them. But since so

Medallion gol farangi, Karabagh, wool on wool, late nineteenth century, 6'7" × 4'11" (Ref. 1539)

Karabagh is the region of the huge province of Azerbaijan which straddles the present borders of the Soviet Union and Iran, a border which until this century had considerable flexibility, not surprising given the nomadic nature of many of its inhabitants. Thus many of the rugs attributed to the Karabagh have either a marked Caucasian, i.e. non-Iranian, flavour or they seem closer to the Persian weaving style. This charming small rug with a central quatrefoil medallion and *gol farangi* pattern of roses in Western taste is clearly Persian; although *gol farangi* rugs are known from the Caucasus, both the colour and the main border design of this rug are totally uncharacteristic of Caucasian weaving.

Opposite –
All over herati design, Tabriz, wool on cotton, twentieth century, signed: Ijadi, 12'6" × 9'8" (Ref. 1608)
Ijadi was one of the best known twentieth-century Tabrizi *ustads*. This elegant example of his work has a beautifully drawn *herati* pattern on a pink ground and a delightful, pale pistachio-coloured border with a beautifully drawn version of the 'turtle palmette' repeat. Very fine in quality, colouring and weave.

Moghan Ganjeh, the Caucasus, wool on cotton, early twentieth century, 10'9" × 3'6" (Ref. 565)
The presence of cotton in the foundation argues a west Caucasian origin and an attribution to the most famous weaving region there, Kazak. It may be from Moghan or perhaps even from Shirvan, since the design, large medallions called 'Memling *guls*' after the fifteenth-century Flemish painter in whose works such rugs appear, appears on rugs woven all over the Caucasus, as well as on examples from Persia and Central Asia.

many factories were owned by private companies or by rich landlords, such attempts were futile. Their use was largely restricted by the desire of certain factory owners to produce rugs of good quality with wool dyed in the traditional way; the wealthy Bakhtiari *khans*, for example, who owned most of the carpet workshops in the Chahar Mahall Valley west of Esfahan, could afford the best materials and surprisingly few Chahar Mahall rugs contain synthetic dyes, even those made well into the twentieth century.

Unfortunately, very few of Persia's great historic carpets remained in the country. A small number, such as the 'Ardebil' carpets, were exported at the end of the nineteenth century, but even at this time the majority of Persian carpets surviving from the sixteenth and seventeenth centuries were either in Western collections or in Turkey, where they had been preserved in thousands of mosques but were sold off to Western dealers at around the turn of the century. Thus Persian weavers initially had few examples of their great heritage to learn from. However, from the 1890s onwards many lavish portfolios of colour reproductions of great carpets were published in Europe and these served as models for carpet workshops all over Persia.

With careful nurturing, the industry rebuilt its reputation, and trade flourished. New weaving centres were established, and existing ones grew. Carpet weaving became the largest industry in the country.

In 1979 the Shah of Iran was deposed in a violent struggle, and the old order was replaced with a new religious government. Iran, like all the Middle Eastern countries, has always been a turbulent state, yet its creative heritage has survived. This recent upheaval, however, has destabilized the economy to such an extent that many weavers are being forced to give up their traditional profession for better paid work. Economic forces, it seems, may destroy this ancient art form in a way that countless centuries of fierce invaders never could.

CHAPTER TWO

IN A FAR AWAY LAND

I ran is in many ways an inhospitable land. Temperatures in this barren and arid terrain alternate between burning heat and freezing cold. The country is very dry and depends largely on melting snow from the mountains and man-made irrigation systems to maintain the relatively small area of land suitable for agriculture.

As a result, villages and towns have formed around the sites of oases where the land could be farmed quite easily, but of necessity a large part of the population was traditionally nomadic. These people migrated with the seasons, constantly searching for fresh pasture land for the herds of sheep and goats which formed the backbone of their economy. These herds supplied them with meat, milk and, of course, wool which was either traded in its raw state or woven into carpets.

Even today there are still many nomadic tribes, now passionately defending their traditional way of life despite attempts by the government to encourage them to settle. They share the Islamic faith and a daily struggle against the hardships of the land. However, their insular way of life has created tribal cultures which are in many ways quite different from each other. These differences are perhaps more clearly seen in their carpet weaving traditions than in any other part of their day-to-day lives.

The Persian people are born with a love of pattern and colour, perhaps as a reaction against the barren land in which they live, and they pour much of their artistic skill into the weaving of

Opposite –
Mihrab, Tabriz, silk on silk, late nineteenth century, 5′5″ × 4′0″ (Ref. 1618)
Both in colour and design, this pleasing, small prayer rug is wholly characteristic of Tabriz carpet weaving towards the end of the nineteenth century. The rusty red is particularly characteristic of the Tabriz style, while the delicacy of the drawing marks it out from silk rugs woven nearby in the Heriz area (Tabriz and Heriz silk rugs from the turn of the century are often confused in carpet literature). The design of an elaborate vase with a huge bouquet of flowers was one of the most popular compositions within the *mihrab* or prayer arch of Persian prayer rugs of this period.

Sarouk, wool on cotton, late nineteenth century, 9′11″ × 6′10″ (Ref. 1606)
The style and colour of this rug is typical of Sarouk weaving from the late nineteenth century onwards, a style of palette which had enormous influence on 'revivalist' Persian weaving from the 1870s to the 1930s. This rug has a particularly bold design and the unusual emerald green corner pieces are worth noting. Also noteworthy is the uneven side of this carpet, showing the primitive way in which it was made.

23

Qashqa'i women (Robert Harding)

carpets. The elements of the patterns they weave are very similar throughout the country, but each tribe interprets these basics in a different way. Some families even have a pattern or symbol unique to themselves (similar in essence to the clan tartans of the Scots). Certain colour combinations also predominate in each tribe.

The love of ornament extends to every part of their lives. The women dress themselves in bright colours, with vivid sashes and scarves hung with glittering coins. The horses and camels so necessary to their migratory way of life are decked with woven harnesses, saddle-cloths and enormous pannier bags into which an entire family's possessions can be stowed.

Though the traditional black tents of the nomads may seem as sombre as the landscape from the outside, within the walls they are filled with colour and pattern. Walls and ceilings may be decorated with hangings. Large storage bags which serve as 'cupboards' for clothes, utensils and food are also richly patterned, made either from knotted or *kilim* (woven) pieces. The floor is covered in plain

Medallion, Doroksh, wool on cotton, late nineteenth century, 16'5" × 13'2" (Ref. 464)

Doroksh, one of the leading weaving and marketing centres of the east Persian province of Khorasan, is a small town some 200 miles south of the provincial capital, Mashad. Carpets attributed to it are generally of fine quality although large, room-sized, examples such as the present one, are comparatively unusual. The beautifully drawn ogival cartouche repeat in the borders is particularly noteworthy, while the field medallion and corners contain an elaborate and colourful version of the so-called *herati* pattern.

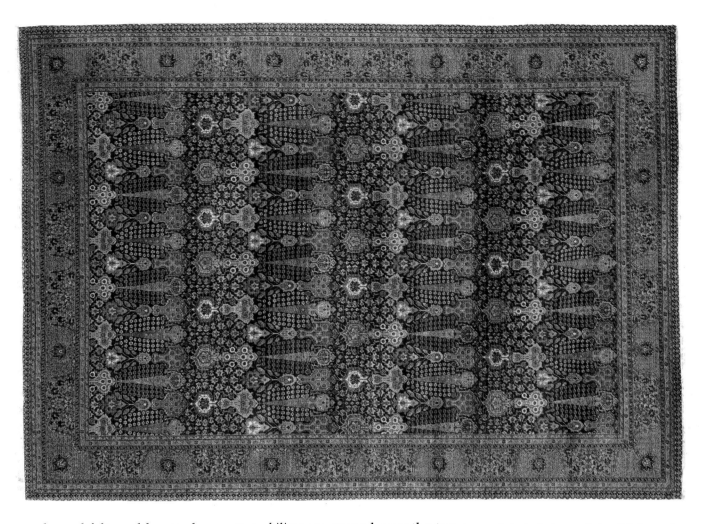

coloured felt, and knotted carpets or *kilims* are spread over the top.

Within town houses, the traditional elongated room shape was enhanced by an arrangement of rugs. One large rug was placed across the top of the room, with narrow runners down either side. Against the walls were cushions made from small rugs with knotted *kilim* backs, so that guests could sit comfortably.

Carpets are not just part of the East's history, they are part of everyday life. Their unique dual function as art form and utilitarian object means that they have great significance in every household, and in village and tribal communities they are as important today as they have ever been. Weavers come from all walks of life, and their skill is highly regarded by their fellow countrymen.

Countless stories and legends emphasize the special place that rugs have in the hearts of the Persian people. It is said that many centuries ago a Persian nobleman was out in the forests hunting gazelle when a great storm blew up. He sought shelter in the house of a farmer, and while he was there fell in love with the man's daughter. Before leaving, he asked the farmer for his daughter's hand in marriage. Despite the suitor's noble lineage, the farmer insisted that he learn a trade before he would give his consent. So the nobleman returned to his father's house and asked the court

Sadagiani all over design Tabriz, wool on cotton, early twentieth century, 10'4" × 7'2" (Ref. 1551)

A dramatic and beautifully coloured Tabriz of some age. Like a number of early twentieth-century Persian carpets, it seems to owe its design in part to a pair of well-known seventeenth century carpets in the 'vase' technique attributed to Kerman, one in Vienna and the other in the Rijksmuseum, Amsterdam. Illustrations of many old rugs were published in lavish volumes around the turn of the century, these reproductions then serving as models for weavers all over the East.

Bakhtiari, gol farangi, Chahar Mahall, wool on cotton, twentieth century, 8'6" × 5'3" (Ref. 1138)
The *gol farangi* pattern became popular all over the Caucasus and Persia during the second half of the nineteenth century. In this example, it is used in a way particularly associated with the Chahar Mahall workshops west of Esfahan, owned by the Bakhtiari *khans*. The principal motifs, large 'cabbage' roses, are contained within a formal arrangement of rectangles and are both within and surrounding the central medallion. The overall composition may well owe something to Western carpets, particularly those of Savonnerie and Aubusson, from which the *gol farangi* pattern derives.

weavers to teach him all they knew, and in this way won the farmer's daughter for himself. Years later, he was captured by a tribe of fierce invaders from whom there seemed no hope of release. To pass the time he wove a rug of great beauty which told the story of his plight. When it was finished he persuaded one of the jailers to take the rug to his father, with the promise of a large reward. When his father saw the rug he gathered an army together, defeated the invaders and released his son. So the nobleman owed his life to the humble farmer, and to the art of weaving.

In tribes and villages, children begin to get involved in the carpet-making process from as early an age as four years old. Their first job will be to help their mothers spinning and preparing the wool. Since the loom is set up in the house in winter, and close by outside in summer, during every waking hour they will be surrounded by carpets.

At about the age of six, by watching her mother work, and helping to prepare the looms, a child is ready to start her first small carpet. People from the West sometimes express concern that children start work so young, but in the East it is considered part of the education process. Indeed, as an artistic training it is little different from a European youngster going to piano lessons or dancing classes.

Often the finest carpet a tribal woman ever weaves is begun when she is about eleven years old. This is the age when Iranian girls and those from many other weaving countries in the East are considered ready for marriage (though historically they may sometimes have been as young as nine). Marriages are arranged by the parents, and it is not unusual for the boy and girl to meet for the first time at the wedding ceremony. Although the concept of a romantic match is largely unheard of, the prospective groom's

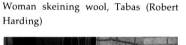
Woman skeining wool, Tabas (Robert Harding)

parents are keen to establish that their daughter-in-law will be a good homemaker. As part of the marriage negotiations, the bride's father will display the rug his daughter has been working on for her dowry. He points to its skilled craftsmanship and artistic merits as an indication of his daughter's character. This rug is in a sense the girl's 'diploma' for marriage, illustrating her good taste and tidy work. The great effort which goes into the making of a bridal rug means it is highly valued in the market place.

Baluchi children (Robert Harding)

For the first few years after a girl is married she makes rugs to supply specific needs, for her children and for her home. Carpets are piled up to make beds, laid on the floor as a 'table' or sewn into cushions and bags. Her husband's taste will also begin to show in her work. This is particularly noticeable when a girl from one tribe marries into another tribe. She will often choose the size and colouring of her rugs according to the traditions of her home tribe, but the details of pattern may well derive from her husband's tribe, perhaps incorporating symbols or colours which are specific to his family. The originality of these rugs can add to their value, and certainly adds to their charm.

Sometimes both husband and wife will work together on the same carpet. An expert can spot harder areas where the knots have been pulled tight with a man's strength, and softer areas which the woman has worked on. In addition, although there are only two basic kinds of knot, it is possible to spot slight variations in knotting technique by which the origin of a rug can be decided with amazing accuracy.

Once the specific needs of the household have been satisfied, the woman continues to weave. Tribal people do not use banks or savings schemes, even today. Instead they build up stores of carpets which can be sold off to raise capital as specific needs arise. The weavers do not work with the intention of selling immediately. Carpets are usually kept (and used), or rolled aside for at least ten

Medallion gol farangi, Karabagh, wool on wool, early twentieth century, 7'0" × 3'11" (Ref. 569)

Another stylized rendition of the *gol farangi* design with two large medallions conjoined by a diamond surrounded by roses and lilies. The palette is also typical of rugs in this design from north-west Persia. There is a poorly written inscription and date each side of the field but this is not legible.

All over design, Sarouk, wool on cotton, late nineteenth century, 10'2" × 6'8" (Ref. 1346)

A handsome Sarouk of rich colouring and design made with fine quality silky wool. The beautifully combined colours of the deep blue field, with the floral 'diamond' arabesques, and an unusual integrated border make it one of the finest examples of Sarouk weaving.

years before it finally becomes necessary to sell them and in fact they will be worth more after many years of hard service than they were when newly woven. When the time comes, the carpet is taken to the nearest town and sold in the bazaar there. Occasionally, when a rug of particular significance has to be sold the weaver may impose certain conditions – that the carpet be cherished, that it be kept until real necessity forces it to be sold again – before he will agree to part with the carpet. The agreement may even be backed by a curse which will blight the purchaser if he breaks the conditions.

City rugs are a rather different case. These are not produced in the home, but in so-called factories (or, more accurately, workshops, since all work is still done by hand). These carpets are produced specifically for sale, and their size, colour and design will be dictated by the fashions of the time. For example, the traditional shades of colour often seem harsh to the Western eye, so they may be consciously abandoned in favour of softer tones to increase their marketability.

The factory weavers are paid weekly or monthly, and are overseen by a supervisor. He checks the quality of their work and may even call out details of the pattern as the weavers sit in rows before their looms. To foreigners this may sound like a simple song, but the 'lyrics' are probably "one red, three yellow, one blue." If he considers an area of knotting to be inferior he will undo it and knot it again. This close attention to detail means that he can only oversee two or three looms at most. In the bigger workshops,

Carpet Factory, Mahan (Robert Harding)

Medallion, Heriz, wool on cotton, late nineteenth century, 13'0" × 10'0" (Ref. 1558)
This is a beautiful and, in design terms, unusual example of Heriz weaving. Having said that, it should be emphasized that rugs attributed to Heriz and its environs (Heriz itself is a town some 70 miles to the east of Tabriz) are known under a variety of names, some of which are, geographically, quite meaningless but which have become accepted in the international carpet trade as indicating a particular quality. Without elaborating on this, suffice to say that a great Heriz, whatever that attribution is taken to mean, is a very splendid thing, as this carpet shows.

Weaving, Esfahan (Robert Harding)

therefore, there are a number of supervisors, each responsible for a number of looms. They work independently, and it is not unheard of for a weaver fired by one overseer to be taken on by another within the same workshop.

The final category of weavers are the fine craftsmen. They also work in the cities, but with looms set up in their own homes or private workshops. The carpets they produce are works of art in their own right, often signed by the weaver, and these skilfully woven items command the highest prices.

The work is intense and time-consuming. It can take years to finish a carpet. Wages, however, are low, and especially since the war in Iran many weavers have given up their profession to work for higher wages rebuilding the shattered cities. As a result, fewer and fewer carpets are now being produced. Consequently, prices are spiralling as demand far exceeds supply.

Tribal carpet makers are less affected by these economic trends than the village and city weavers. The tribal peoples are still largely self-sufficient. Their tents are their homes and few have electricity, most households still depending on oil lamps for light and open fires for cooking. Their food comes from the animals they take with them on their travels, the wool they weave is sheared from their own sheep, and the dyes the carpet is coloured with are gathered from the plants which they gather along their way.

But for the majority of weavers, Western-style economics are increasingly important. It is not just the Western collector who is beginning to suffer as a result of this. It remains to be seen what the effect of these trends will be on a people who have grown up surrounded by carpets and the artistic traditions which go with them.

Pictorial, Karabagh, wool on cotton, early twentieth century, 6'3" × 4'5" (Ref. 577)
Although tentatively ascribed to the northern province of Karabagh, it is possible that this rug may have been woven further south, perhaps in the Bijar region, to which other examples similar in design, drawing and colour have been attributed. Something of a mystery but charming for all that.

Bazaar, Esfahan (Robert Harding)

Medallion, Malayer, wool on cotton, early twentieth century, 16'5" × 7'8" (Ref. 1573)

Long rugs of this overall design are associated in particular with Bidjar but were made elsewhere, as this example demonstrates. Its palette is typical of Malayer and its wide outer brown 'frame' is a well-known characteristic of Hamadan weaving. An interesting feature of this carpet is the use of *ton sur ton*, here pink on red, for the subtle field pattern of interlocking hexagons. Notice the use of the *herati* pattern in the blue ground corners, something else one would not expect to find on a Bidjar version but which is typical of Malayer weaving.

Bakhtiari Tree of Life, Chahar Mahall, probably Shahr Kord, wool on cotton, late nineteenth century, 21'6" × 14'7" (Ref. 361).

Experts on the history of the Bakhtiari and their weaving have made the following observations on this carpet: "This is one of the most brilliant examples of Chahar Mahall weaving we have seen and its quality makes the absence of an inscription surprising. For practical reasons, large white or yellow ground carpets are comparatively rare, yet they seem to have been particularly prized by the Bakhtiari Great Khans, for whose splendid palaces in the Chahar Mahall Valley many of the largest and most beautiful examples were woven. The cypress tree was a favourite motif among Bakhtiari weavers, although it can seldom have been used to such powerful effect as here. The colourful and ornate main border design, apparently based on the *boteh* motif, is most unusual."

Overleaf left –

Medallion, Tabriz, wool on cotton, early twentieth century, 22'0" × 15'3" (Ref. 1578)

A brilliantly coloured and well drawn Tabriz medallion carpet, the work of the *ustad* Hajji Jalili. Even the 'turtle' palmettes in the main borders, a traditional pattern on weavings from this area and often considered to be of Kurdish origin, are rendered in an unusually graceful and colourful manner. The vivid open red field around the central medallion makes the latter stand out with particular clarity and we should note the elegance of the 'split-palmettes' or *rumi* which outline both the central medallion and the corners.

right –

All over gol farangi, Bijar, wool on cotton, late nineteenth century, 20'0" × 13'3" (Ref. 1570)

Although structurally typical of weavings from Bijar, neither the colour nor the design of this carpet are usual. The dark blue field is covered with offset rows of large and small medallions, the largest of which contain roses – the pattern known as *gol farangi*. A rare carpet for its quality and colouring.

CHAPTER THREE

UNRAVELLING THE TALE

L ittle has changed in the art of carpet making since the earliest weavers discovered by trial and error how to create a piled fabric from a network of knots.

As the craft of a travelling people the materials and equipment used by weavers were, of necessity, simple. The majority of carpets have always been made of wool shorn from the tribe's flocks, washed in a stream and dried in the sun, although sometimes goat or camel hair is incorporated, particularly on the edges of a carpet, for greater strength.

In the remote villages and nomadic tribes, carding the wool for spinning is often one of the first household chores given to a child. The prepared wool is then spun on simple spindles by the old women of the tribe, and dyed in a myriad of shades using plant, animal and mineral dyes. Liquid sheep dung was traditionally used as a mordant, to set the dyes and make the colours brighter and longer lasting. This method is still used today in the more remote areas, though in towns and cities almost all wool is now dyed synthetically, so this 'setting' process is no longer necessary. However, the switch to man-made colours is one of the few technical developments in a craft which has been practised for more than twenty-five centuries.

Opposite –
The Story of Joseph, Ravar Kerman, wool on cotton, c.1900, 7'7" × 4'8" (Ref. 717) This charming rug is typical of pictorial weaving produced in Kerman and the adjacent village of Ravar in the late nineteenth and early twentieth centuries; many of the compositions are derived from European prints which were very popular in Qajar Persia. Here the story of Joseph and his brothers is told. We can see Joseph inside the whale (*centre*), Joseph being sold (*above*) and Benjamin being handed by Jacob to his brother Judah (*below*).

All over design, Esfahan, wool and silk on silk, twentieth century, signed: Abbas Mansouri, 5'7" × 3'7" (Ref. 865) Many of the most beautiful and memorable Esfahan weavings of the late Pahlavi period are by important master weavers who proudly signed their work and whose styles were, and are, easily recognizable by Persian connoisseurs. This example has a design of floral wreaths containing vividly coloured flower sprays with birds.

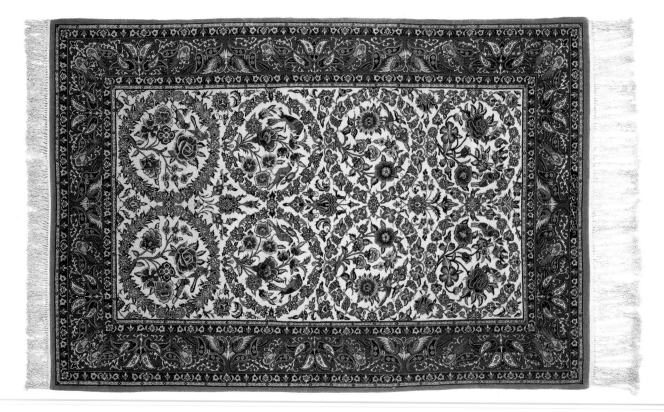

I do not include the production of machine-made carpets here, since a true oriental rug is worked entirely by hand. Machine-made rugs are easily recognizable since the pattern is indistinct, or even invisible, on the reverse. These rugs are not actually knotted: strands are simply looped around the warp threads and can easily be pulled out using tweezers. They are slightly cheaper than real orientals, but do not wear well, have no investment value and cannot even be compared with hand-woven pieces.

The nomads have always used collapsible looms so that an unfinished carpet can simply be rolled up and moved on to the next camp site when necessary. These looms consist of two straight beams, usually no longer than an arm's length, tied to four sturdy pegs driven into the ground to create a basic frame. The warp (vertical) threads are stretched out between the two poles as close together as possible. The more densely packed these threads are, the finer will be the final knot count of the carpet. The tribal women kneel on the ground to work, threading the first weft (horizontal) threads in and out to form a sturdy *kilim* woven border. This *kilim* can be plain or patterned, according to the taste of the weaver and the traditions of her tribe.

After an inch or so has been woven, the first line of knots is begun. The nimble fingers of the weaver pass a single strand round two, or more rarely three or four, warp threads, and pull the knot tight. There are two basic kinds of knot. The Turkish, or Ghiordes, knot is made by laying a strand over two warp threads, passing the ends round the outside of the two warps, then pulling them back up through the middle. The Persian, or Senneh, knot is worked by passing one end of the strand around a single warp thread, then over and under the adjacent thread.

The type of knot used in a carpet bears no relation to its quality

Opposite –
Bakhtiari garden design, Chahar Mahall, Shalamzar, wool on cotton, first quarter of the twentieth century, Inscribed: *Farmayesh Amirza Abbas valad sadegh Hajji Zeinal Shalamzari* ('By Order of Amirza Abbas, true son of Hajji Zeinal of Shalamzar'), 15'1" × 10'6" (Ref. 155)
Such carpets as this, although not always of better quality than those made without inscriptions, were quite clearly intended for the personal use of the rich *khans* or merchants who ordered them. The present inscription indicates that the carpet was not made for one of the Bakhtiari Great Khans but is still of interest since it indicates the exact place of weaving, the town of Shalamzar.

All over design, Nain, wool and silk on cotton, twentieth century, 8'11" × 5'3" (Ref. 863)
It is surprising how what might be thought of as the limited range of colours associated with the typical Nain palette can be used to such varied effect. This example has a rare design of two forms of lobed medallion arranged on the diagonal axis on a dark-blue field. Within each medallion are stylized arrangements of floral bouquets which are echoed on the field between the medallions. A rug of considerable elegance.

Amamdwal sheep range (Robert Harding)

or value, but it can be a useful guide as to where the carpet was made. The names Turkish and Persian knot are in fact something of a misnomer, since both are used in Iran and elsewhere in the Middle East. In the earliest days of carpet weaving the names may well have been precise, but since then the two knots have spread far afield as nation has invaded nation and persecuted tribes have fled to different parts of the continent, taking their weaving traditions with them. To further confuse the issue, Senneh, the alternative name for the Persian knot, is in fact a weaving town which uses the

Medallion, Kashan, wool on cotton, early twentieth century, 6'7" × 4'5" (Ref. 567) In the late nineteenth and early twen-tieth centuries, the central Persian city of Kashan was, as it had been under the Safavid Shahs three to four hundred years earlier, one of the great weaving centres. It was renowned for rugs of the highest quality and originality and this extraordinary example, with its delicate drawing and brilliant contrasts of colour, is typical of Kashan inventiveness. It is interesting, however, that the main bor-der, both in colour and style, is influ-enced by Sarouk weaving.

Turkish knot. Although there are really only two basic knots, there are, however, minute differences from tribe to tribe in the way these knots are tied. Although almost impossible for the untrained eye to see, to an expert these variations provide yet another clue as to the origins of a particular rug.

Though most weavers tie knots with their fingers, some use a

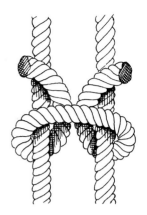

Turkish or Ghiordes knot

Persian or Senneh knot

All over gol farangi, Senneh, wool on silk, early twentieth century, 6'4" × 4'2" (Ref. 1613)

This Senneh piled rug is particularly noteworthy for having multi-coloured silk warps arranged in chromatic bands; this rare feature is also sometimes encountered on Senneh silk *kilims* as well as on silk rugs from Kashan. The elegantly designed field has a particularly successful rendering of the *gol farangi* pattern.

hooked knife, called a *tikh*, to pull the ends of the yarn through the warp threads. The blade of the knife is used to trim the yarn after the knot has been tied. After one row of knots has been completed they are vigorously beaten down with a *daftun*, a comb-like tool, to create a firm fabric. The knots are held in place with one or two weft threads, woven in and out, followed by another row of knots.

In this way the work progresses slowly. After a few inches

Opposite –
Mihrab, Kashan, wool on cotton, late nineteenth – early twentieth century, 14'1" × 10'2" (Ref. 1563)
Rugs in this distinctive design have been made in most of the principal weaving centres of Persia throughout the twentieth century. The field, of course, is based on the *mihrab* or 'prayer arch' although the size of this carpet indicates that it was not intended for devotional use.

Qulyahi, wool on cotton, late nineteenth – early twentieth century, 19'10" × 11'8" (Ref. 1130)
Qulyahi is, or was, an area to the west of Hamadan, the principal town of which is Songur. In many respects this splendid carpet is typical of Hamadan weaving, in particular its colour and the presence of a plain outer brown 'frame'. In other ways, particularly the overall design, it strikes one immediately as close to Bijar medallion carpets. Its exact attribution is slightly controversial although the one suggested here seems reasonable.

have been completed, the trailing ends are trimmed back to about two inches, allowing the pattern to be appreciated for the first time. This pattern is worked from memory by tribal and village weavers. The geometric elements of the patterns are handed down by word of mouth from mother to daughter, but combined and interpreted according to the taste of the individual.

The pattern develops as the weaver works, much as a musician may create a tune according to his feelings. The design often incorporates those possessions dear to the weaver's heart, the chickens, birds and dogs which are central to tribal life. In addition, there are specific motifs, each unique to a particular family, which the weavers of that family will include in their work. Thus every carpet is slightly different, even if made by the same weaver, since the pattern is decided as she progresses.

In the larger towns and cities the process is slightly different. Here the looms are permanent structures built upright. They are constructed from two solid vertical posts with crossbeams at top and bottom. Contrary to the custom in nomadic rug-making, cotton is usually used for warp and weft threads, since it is stronger than wool. The weaving technique is, however, exactly the same, though rather than working from memory, these weavers use a carefully painted diagram, or cartoon.

All over design, Nain, wool and silk on cotton, mid-twentieth century, signed: Iran–Nain–Soltani, 14′8″ × 10′5″ (Ref. 147)

The Soltani workshop was one of the best known in Nain during the reign of Muhammad Reza Shah Pahlavi in the decades following World War II. As is often the case, areas of white are piled in silk to give a greater depth and lustre to the surface. Here, somewhat unusually for a Nain, an elaborate all-over *herati* pattern has been used for the field.

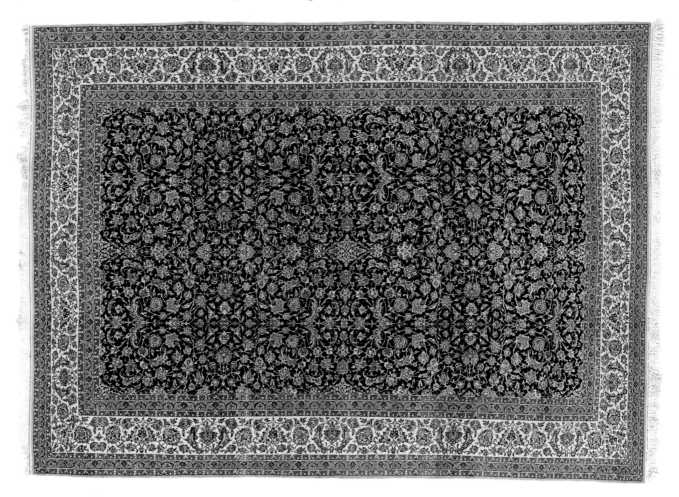

Omar Khayam, Esfahan, wool and silk, mid-twentieth century, signed: Iran–Esfahan–Sadeghe–Sirafian, 3'7" × 2'8" (Ref. 1018)

This tiny and finely woven mat, from the greatest Esfahan *ustad* of the late Pahlavi period, Sirafian, has a pictorial scene based on Persian manuscript illustration of the sixteenth century and is based on the poem *Wine, Women and Song* by Omar Khayam. A Sufi saint is shown seated and being served by acolytes, one of whom, at the top right, wears the 'stick' turban which appears in so many early sixteenth-century Persian paintings and can also be found on hunting carpets of the same period. A very fine rug based on a silk background and with a silk fringe.

Wool, Esfahan (Robert Harding)

These cartoons are produced by professional artists, who work either for a factory, or in the bazaars. Cartoons vary in price according to their complexity, and whether they are new or have been woven before. A new and detailed pattern can cost as much as one month's salary. However, the first carpet woven from a new pattern will be worth many times more than a carpet based on an older pattern. The cartoons not only specify pattern, but colour as well, and the artist may well help the weaver to choose the shades of yarn to be used. However, once work is under way the weaver usually cannot resist adding some elements of her own. As a result, however many carpets are produced from the same cartoon they are very unlikely to be identical, even if woven by the same person.

The town weaver sits on a bench before her loom with the balls of coloured yarn hung from the warp threads above her head. The pattern is pinned below them, where it can be easily referred to. As

All over design, Qashqa'i, south-west Persia, Fars, wool on wool, early twentieth century, 8'4" × 5'4" (Ref. 1204)
The attribution of this rug to the Qashqa'i is by no means certain, although it was almost certainly made in Fars. The dark wool foundations, the end finishes and the colour all suggest that an attribution to either the Khamseh or Luri is equally possible, while the particular way the red lattice with its white outlining is drawn is associated in particular with the Afshars. Note how in the outer guard on the right long side, the design changes half-way down to the familiar blue and white 'block' repeat. A very interesting and unusual tribal rug.

the carpet grows, the bench may be raised before the loom, or the warp threads loosened so that the lower section of the carpet can be rolled away. If the bench is raised, then as the carpet nears completion, the weaver will be perched many feet in the air with her head almost touching the ceiling.

When eventually the carpet is completed, the knots are held in place with another band of *kilim*, and then the carpet is cut from the loom. The trailing ends of the warp threads form the tassles on either end of the carpet, often left longer at the top than the bottom. These may either be left smooth, or be knotted into braided tassles.

After months of work, the carpet will inevitably have become rather dirty, so it is taken to a fast-flowing stream, where the accumulated grime can be washed away. The carpet is left out in the sun until it is completely dry, and it is then ready for the final stage.

The carpet is taken to the master shearer. He works with a large flat blade of incredible sharpness, gently shaving away the pile of the carpet to give a smooth, even finish. This is a nerve-wracking and highly skilled process, one tiny slip of the knife could

Medallion, Bibikabad, wool on cotton, first quarter of the twentieth century, 13'6" × 11'2" (Ref. 146)

Bibikabad is one of several well-known villages in the Hamadan weaving area of northern Persia. Rugs given this specific nomenclature usually rely for their decorative effect on elaborations of either the *herati* pattern (as used here) or the *boteh*. The appearance of very large corners, which create the effect of a medallion within a medallion, in this case ivory on dark blue, is also consistent with such an attribution.

destroy months of hard work. Once the trimming is completed, the carpet may be pressed using a huge flat iron and damp cotton cloths to smooth out any wrinkles and make the pile lie flat.

These beautifully finished pieces with knotted piles are what most people think of as Persian carpets. However, before weavers discovered the art of knotting, they made flat woven pieces, or *kilims*, and these are still produced today.

We tend to associate *kilims* – flat-woven rugs in what is called the slit-tapestry technique – exclusively with the tribal or small village weaving community. This is, of course, not historically accurate; in Safavid Persia during the sixteenth and seventeenth centuries, wonderful silk *kilims* were woven in the same Imperial workshops in Kashan and Esfahan which produced pile rugs, and the wonderfully sophisticated Senneh wool *kilims* of the late eighteenth and early nineteenth centuries, although made by Kurdish weavers, could hardly be described as 'tribal'. Nevertheless, many of the most beautiful Persian *kilims* of the last 150 years were made by various tribes, those of the Qashqa'i of Fars being particularly famous.

Though their lack of pile means they are not as warm or hard-wearing as knotted pieces, they are a great deal quicker and easier to produce. They are also lighter, and hence easier to transport, and double-faced. In the East they are not generally used as floor coverings, but as wall hangings, bed covers, bags and cushion backs. They are produced by weaving weft threads in and out of the warp. The patterns are created using different coloured threads, the coloured strands carried backwards and forwards only so far as the design dictates. As a result there are small 'holes' in the rugs where blocks of different colours meet. These are almost

Opposite –
Persian Qashqa'i, Senneh and Russian Bessarabian kilims, wool on cotton and wool on wool, twentieth century (Ref. Kilims).

Medallion, Sarouk, wool on cotton, early twentieth century, 5'11" × 4'5" (Ref. 642) Sarouk is the principal weaving town of one of the most important carpet-making areas in Iran, Fereghan. This rug has a stylized *herati* pattern on its dark blue ground, a form of decoration much associated with Fereghan weaving. The central large ivory ground medallion is a stylized version of the *gol farangi* pattern.

Carpet washing at Rey, Teheran (Robert Harding)

invisible in well produced pieces, and may be eliminated by working each coloured weft thread round one common warp thread where two areas meet.

Another well-known type of flat-woven rug is the *sumakh*, a form of brocading; these are associated primarily with Caucasian village weavers and with the Shahsavan tribe of the northern Persian province of Azerbaijan.

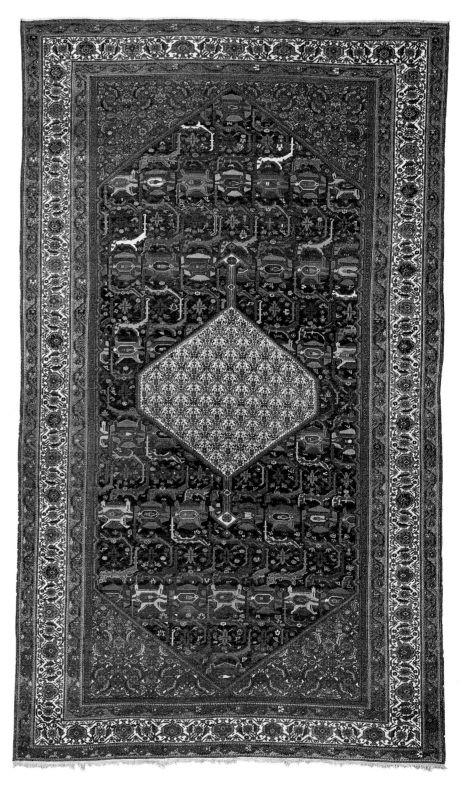

Medallion, Malayer, wool on cotton, c.1900, 19'9" × 11'7" (Ref. 366)
Although the town of Malayer and its surrounding district is in the Hamadan area of northern Persia, its weavings are quite distinct and the finest of them are held in high regard. This is a most unusual carpet in which a conventional 'medallion and corners' composition has been overlaid on a brilliantly coloured repeat design which seems to owe more to tribal weaving than to the town workshop.

Like *kilims*, *sumakhs* have no pile, though they do tend to be tougher and more tightly woven. They are produced using a basic network of warp and weft threads, but additional coloured weft threads are woven into this framework in short strands to create the pattern, and the ends are left trailing on the reverse of the piece. As a result, *sumakhs* are not reversible in the way that *kilims* are, since the back is a thick shaggy mass of wool creating an insulating layer which makes them considerably warmer than straightforward flat woven pieces.

Despite the diversity of weaving techniques, they are united by the incredible creative talents of Persian weavers, who turn them from objects of everyday use into works of art, and set them apart from the products of other weaving nations, which seem like pale imitations in comparison.

Carpet washing at Rey, Teheran (Robert Harding)

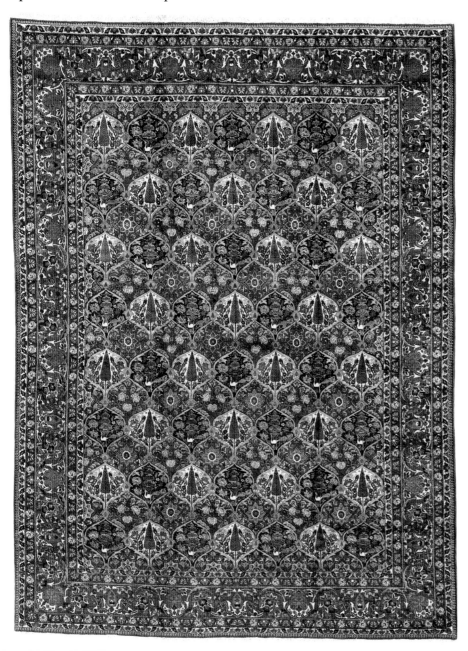

Bakhtiari all over design, Chahar Mahall, probably Shahr Kord, wool on cotton, early twentieth century, 13'9" × 10'2" (Ref. 1087)
This is one of the most famous designs associated with carpets produced in the Chahar Mahall factories owned by the wealthy Bakhtiari *khans* around the turn of the century. The elegant ogival lattice has often been taken to indicate Mughal influence.

CHAPTER FOUR

READING THE PICTURES

Pattern and colour are central to the life of the weavers. They work instinctively, unconsciously drawing on traditions passed by word of mouth, relying on their natural good taste to produce rugs of tremendous beauty.

The colours they use and the patterns they weave are part of the heritage of their tribes and communities. But weaving is a living art, and each carpet reveals as much about the character of the person who made it as it does about the conventions of the craft.

The nomads live day to day, their movements controlled only by the search for fresh pasture. They do not plan their lives and, similarly, they do not plan their rugs. The size of a rug is decided arbitrarily, limited by the size of loom which can be conveniently transported during migration. Patterns are woven on impulse; there is no overall plan, the rug simply evolves. It is finished when it has reached the maximum length allowed by the loom, or when the wool runs out. As a result patterns are sometimes terminated quite abruptly. Often this idiosyncrasy adds to the charm (and value) of a tribal rug, though in extreme cases it can result in a strangely unbalanced piece.

City weavers, in contrast, are part of a society which includes great architects and philosophers. There is nothing haphazard about the way they work. Everything is planned in advance, so that as the weaver ties her first row of knots, she knows exactly what the finished product will look like. Yet, as we have seen, both sets of weavers use the same technique, are aware of the same colour symbolism, and even have some design elements in common.

The ancient skill of weaving carries with it a whole weight of

Opposite –
Emmad Medallion, Tabriz, wool on cotton, mid-twentieth century, 16'0" × 11'9" (Ref. 1560)
Tabriz is particularly well-known for producing carpets which combine Eastern and Western tastes. Here, the concept of a field surrounded by borders, the field with a central medallion and corners, is traditionally Eastern. Yet both the colour and the individual decorative elements clearly betray Western influence, probably the style and colouring of the great nineteenth-century English artist, William Morris.

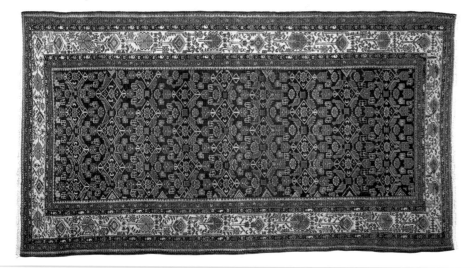

All over design, Malayer, wool on cotton, early twentieth century, 13'1" × 7'0" (Ref. 1575)
Like many village weavings from northwest Persia, those from the Malayer region often take a well-known workshop pattern and render it in a simplified, and quite often very fresh and innovative, way. The design on the dark blue field of this example is probably based on the *herati* pattern but is hardly recognizable now. The side-to-side movement of the shrubs in the ivory ground border is typical of Malayer weaving, as is the palette.

associated symbolism and imagery, but this is largely the province of the Western scholar. To the Persian weaver, these are simply the patterns they have always worked with. If asked the origin of a motif they will explain it in simple terms, with names such as the 'earring' or the 'tree pattern'. These are merely pictorial descriptions, and have little to do with the original significance of a design. Attempts to unravel symbolic meaning are hampered by a lack of documentation, since the history of carpet weaving is an oral tradition.

Opposite –

All over design, Hereke, silk on silk, mid-twentieth century, 5'1" × 3'4" (Ref. 1617)

The silk rugs of Hereke in Turkey are among the finest, in terms of knot count, ever woven. This example is typical of this technical brilliance, having a knot count of around 2,090 knots per square inch. The magnificent design, colouring, quality and size of this rug make it very rare indeed.

Medallion, Tabriz, wool and silk on silk, twentieth century, signed: Azimzadeh–Tagizadeh, 8'3" × 4'11" (Ref. 743)

This rug demonstrates one famous characteristic of twentieth-century Persian weaving, the use of a very small number of colours on a field and borders of one solid colour to give the subtle drawing and flow of the design maximum impact. The most famous group of this type are known as 'five-colour rugs' and here we have an even more minimal but richly successful palette of three shades of coffee on a pale blue ground.

Considering the many thousands of different types of rug produced in Persia, there are surprisingly few basic pattern elements, although each motif will be interpreted in a slightly different way. by every weaving tribe.

The most common pattern is the *herati*. The basic structure of this design is always recognizable in its many variations – a central rosette enclosed in a diamond, with two smaller rosettes at the four corners and an elongated leaf with serrated edges along each side. The motif is also called the *mari* (fish) design. This could mean that the 'leaves' in fact represent stylized fish. Indeed, there is an ancient legend which says that at the time of the full moon the fish of the lakes rise to the surface to admire their reflection – suggesting that *herati* is in fact a neat pictorial motif. Whatever its origins, it appears frequently in rugs from all over Persia.

Other common patterns are the *gol* – Persian for 'flower' –

Opposite –
Tree of Life, Kashan, silk on silk, late nineteenth century, 13'5" × 9'9" (Ref. 419)
An exceptionally elegant silk piled Kashan of unusually large size. Note again the yellow field, a rare and highly prized feature. The great variety of sinuously drawn flowering trees and shrubs in the field, with birds perching among them, recalls Safavid weaving. A rare carpet for its quality and size.

Left –
Nain, wool and silk on cotton, mid-twentieth century, signed: Iran–Habibian, 13'1" × 9'2" (Ref. 1117)
Habibian was the most famous *ustad* in Nain during the late Pahlav period, his best work being considered among the masterpieces of modern Persian weaving. This carpet has the typical palette of Nain weavings but the large and impressive *mihrab* composition is unusual.

Overleaf left –
All over boteh, Tabriz, wool on cotton, mid-twentieth century, 13'4" × 9'8" (Ref. 1049)
We have seen several rugs from different weaving centres with dense all-over *boteh* repeats of great elegance, a design often described in a village context as *boteh mir* and associated with Seraband. There seems little doubt that the concept originated with shawl weavers and was transferred to carpet design after the demise of the Western market for Persian shawls in the mid-nineteenth century.

right –
Shoreshie Medallion, Esfahan, wool and silk, first quarter of the twentieth century, 14'2" × 10'7" (Ref. 1566)
The finest Esfahan carpets from the Pahlavi period, especially those woven on silk foundations, represent for many Iranians their country's supreme modern achievement in carpet weaving art. In both colour and style, this medallion carpet is markedly different from the lovely weavings produced in the decades after World War II and probably dates from the beginning of the 'revival' period in Esfahan weaving during the 1920s.

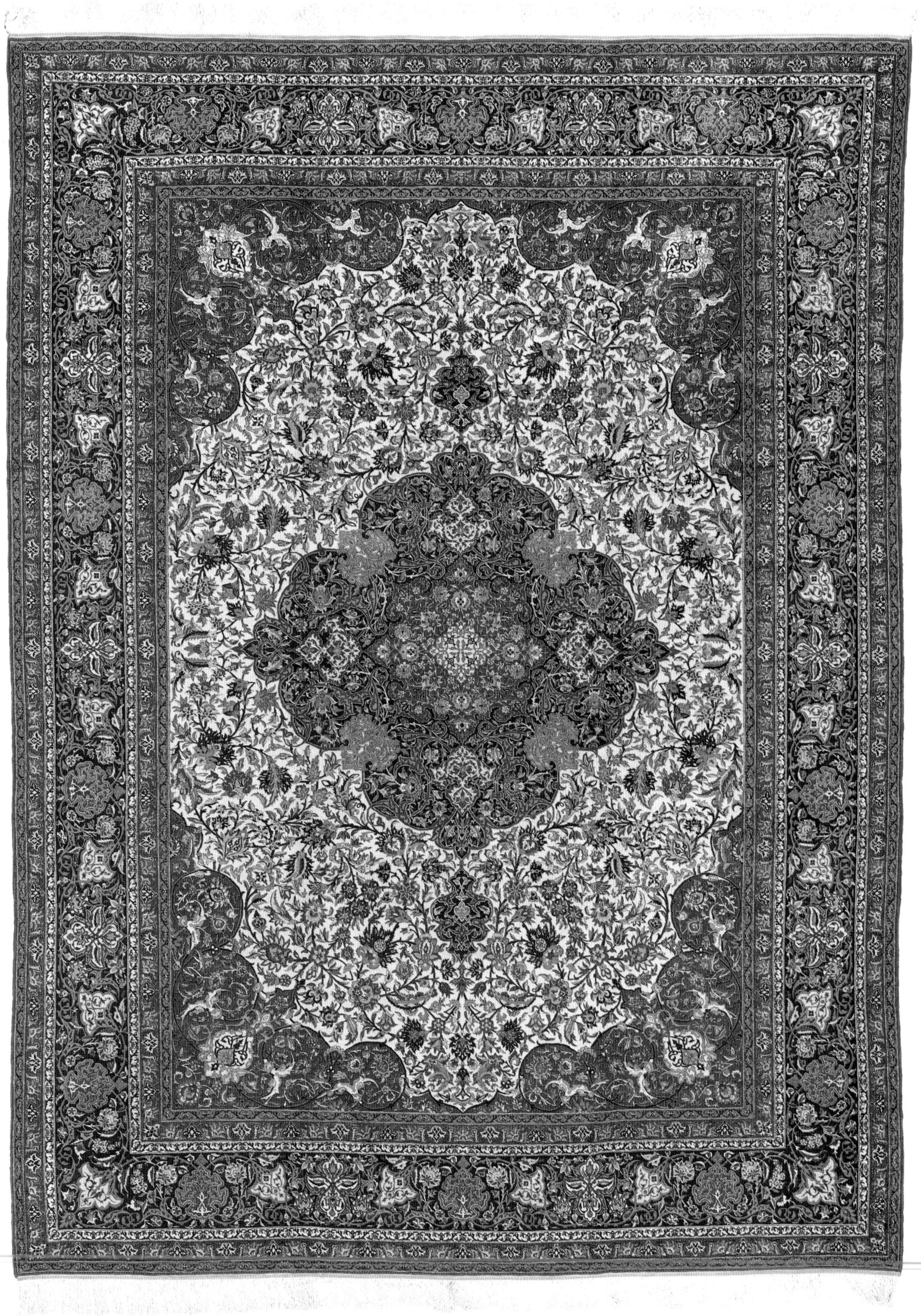

which is a stylized octagonal flower, possibly a rose, and the *boteh*. This is familiar to Westerners as the basic element of the Paisley pattern. It has been variously interpreted as a droplet of water, a stylized almond or a palmetto leaf. *Boteh* means 'leaf' motif and this adds weight to the latter interpretation. Historically, the palmetto leaf was dried and used as a sort of paper for inscribing prayers on, which would explain its frequent inclusion in prayer rugs, and many other carpet designs. The rose is a symbol of the Persian philosophy of life – like life, the rose is beautiful but full of thorns, and once cut eventually withers and dies, mirroring the transience of life. This symbol is particularly popular in rugs from Kashan and Tabriz in Iran, the Karabagh rugs of Russia, and the Savonneries and Aubussons of France.

The palmette is another classical decorative design. Scholars believe it represents the opium poppy which was cultivated, used and abused in Persia from earliest times. For obvious reasons it was traditionally associated with transcendental meditation and mysticism.

In Islamic culture there is not the same distinction between artistic and religious life as there is in the West today. Carpets were, and are, aids to contemplation, even if not specifically prayer rugs, and many designs do have a religious significance.

The prayer rug is one of the most famous Islamic designs and it has enduring popularity with all weavers, from the simple nomadic tribes to the largest city factories. It is, in fact, a very functional item. Every practising Muslim must kneel to pray on clean ground five times a day. In any Muslim country at the prescribed times the streets, shops and houses are filled with men laying down their prayer rugs in the direction of Mecca to do homage to the prophet Mohammed.

Medallion all over design, Khamseh, south-west Persia, Fars, wool on wool, twentieth century, 11'0" × 4'10" (Ref. 505)

The Khamseh Confederation of Fars was formed in 1861–2; unlike all other such tribal confederations it was not based on blood ties but was a grouping of five independent tribes formed by the central government to offset the growing power of the Qashqa'i. The rugs of the two Confederations are often difficult to tell apart but the structure of this rug, including the use of dark brown wool in the foundations, the range of colours and the particular style of decoration found in the series of three-poled hexagonal medallions with their ivory grounds, are all indications of Khamseh rather than Qashqa'i origin.

A prayer rug is instantly recognizable by the *mihrab*, or prayer arch which is its dominant motif, echoing the architecture of the mosques. The shape of the arch is an indication of the weaver's skill. In tribal rugs it is represented simply: two linear columns rise from the base of the rug and then either indent to form a small rectangle at the top, or else slope diagonally inwards to a point. In city rugs the arch is often highly refined, curving in elegant arabesques to its apex. In some rugs a lantern hangs from its centre, suspended by a long chain, and this too echoes the lamps which hang from the ceilings of the mosques. Prayer rugs are particularly popular among the town weavers of Tabriz, Kashan, Esfahan and Qum.

Overleaf –
Dabier-Sanayehe, Medallion Kashan, wool on cotton, late nineteenth – early twentieth century, 19'4" × 11'10" (Ref. 149)
Like the Mashad carpet illustrated on page 145, the field of this rug is also loosely based on the 'Ardebil' design, with a central medallion ringed by palmettes and a hanging lamp at either end, the central medallion and palmettes being quartered in the corners. This is a carpet of considerable technical quality, the elaborate field being almost too much for the eye to comprehend. It is woven with a particularly soft but firm wool associated with Kashan carpets and usually called *kurk*.

Sirafian Medallion, unsigned, Esfahan, wool on silk, mid-twentieth century, 10'6" × 6'11" (Ref. 1550)
Another finely woven example of late Pahlavi period Esfahan weaving distinguished by its use of a silk foundation. Rugs in this particular palette are well-known and quite distinctive to Esfahan. The sinuous movement of the split-palmettes around the central star medallion is very attractive and rugs with this design are sometimes described as having the *eslomie* pattern.

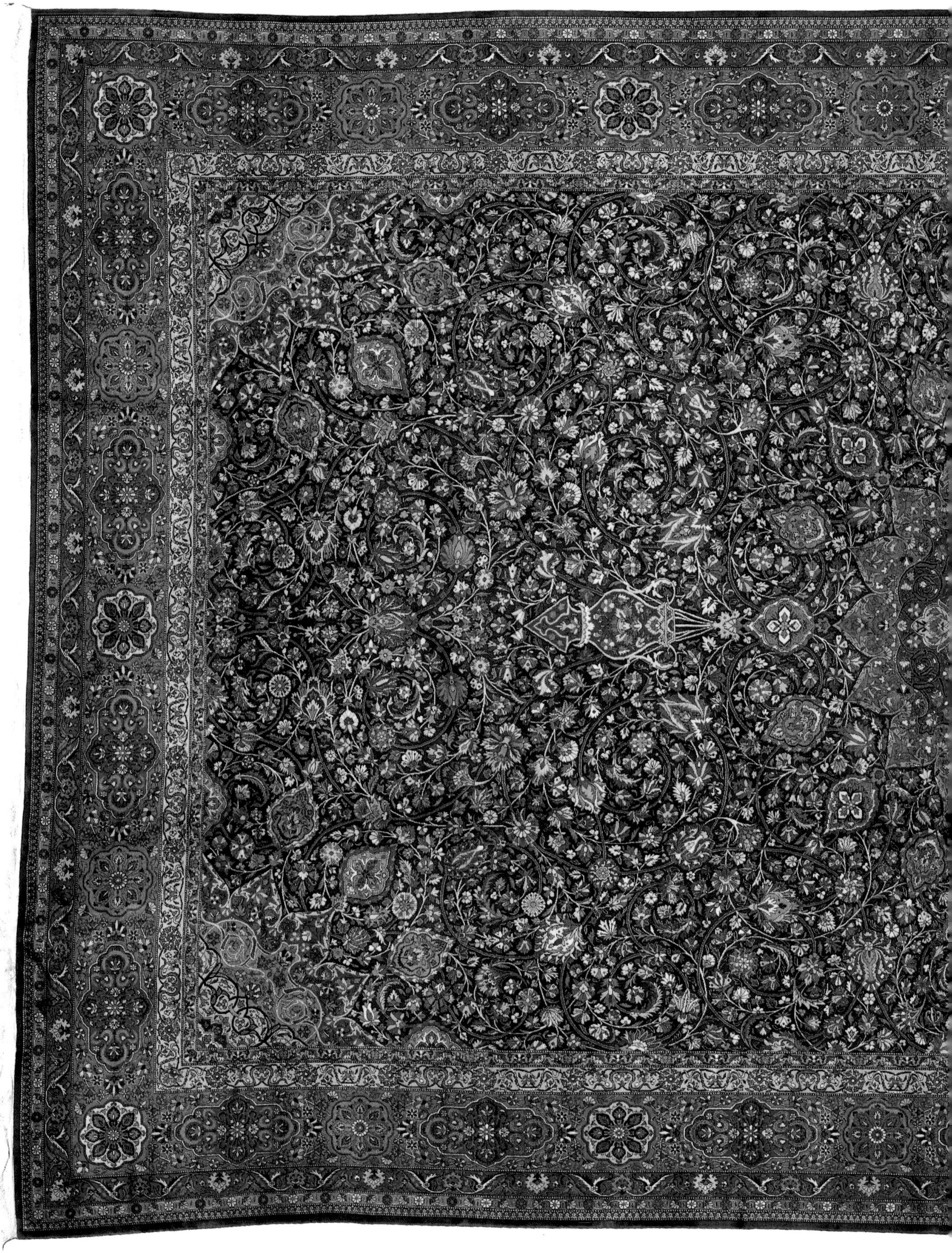

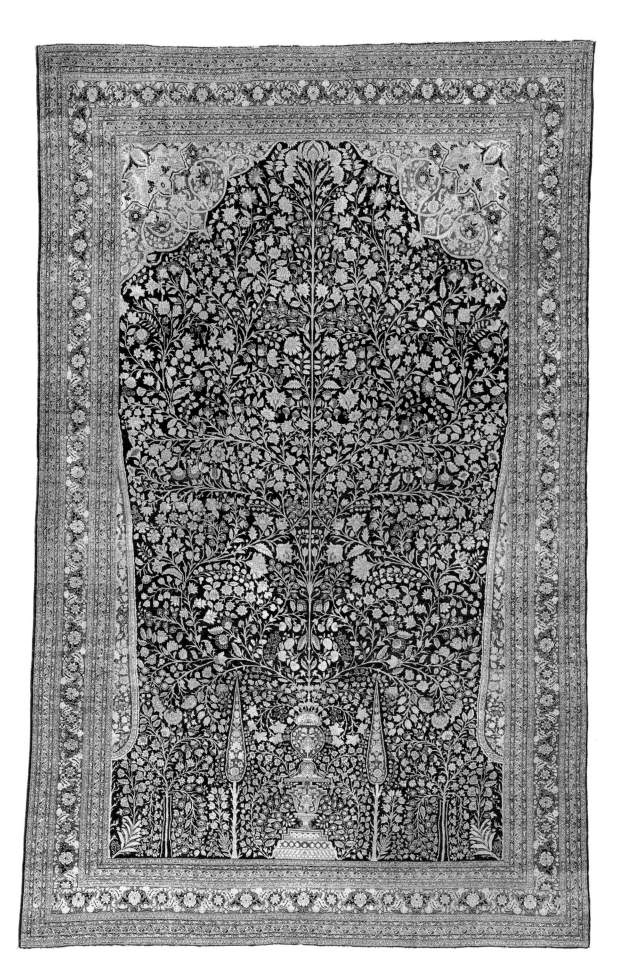

Sometimes a pair of hands is woven into the design on either side of the arch. Opinions as to the significance of this motif vary. Some say it is simply a guide for the worshipper to position himself on the rug. Others argue that the five fingers of the hand represent the five members of the prophet's family – Mohammed himself, his cousin and son-in-law Ali, his daughter Fatima, and their two sons Hasan and Hosein. The motif is often described more simply as 'The Hand of Fatima' and is thought to have talismanic and protective powers. A rake-shaped comb may also be included in the plan. This often indicates that the rug was woven for a poor but pious man, since cleanliness is one of the foremost Muslim virtues.

Though most Persian prayer rugs are decorated with a single *mihrab*, some have a number arranged across their width. These multiple prayer rugs are sometimes woven either for family prayers or for mosques and are much more common in Turkey than in Iran. It is obvious from the smallness of the arches on many such rugs, however, that they were not intended for ritual use; in these instances, the design is often purely decorative and was intended to be displayed on a wall. Rugs with multiple arches are called *safs*.

The *mihrab* is also used on larger carpets to represent the gate of a house, and hence a welcome to visitors. Traditionally, Persian homes often had a window of this shape in the living room overlooking a garden, therefore on these carpets flowers often flourish under the arch. These rugs were often hung on the wall to create an extra 'window' and garden.

There are two simple ways of telling whether a *mihrab* design rug was for prayer or secular enjoyment. The first clue is the size of

Opposite –
Mihrab Tree of Life, Tabriz, wool on cotton, late nineteenth century, 15'9" × 10'0" (Ref. 1565)
This carpet is most unusual for its size and quality, bearing the *mihrab* (prayer arch) design by the *ustad* Hajji Jalili. Hadji Jalili was certainly one of the well-known weavers of the late nineteenth century and the colouring design of this carpet is living evidence of his acknowledged success.

Elephant foot design, Tekke, probably Khorasan, wool on wool, early twentieth century, 5'3" × 4'4" (Ref. 1530)
Rugs of this particular design are associated with the Tekke Turkoman tribe of Central Asia and were often known in the trade as 'Bokharas'. However, many Tekke Turkomans lived in Persia and this example may well have been made there. The colour, predominantly red, is typical of Turkoman weavings and the repeated medallions in the field are called *güls* (Persian *gol*) or 'elephant-foot' design.

the rug – prayer rugs are always small, so they can be easily carried around by the devout. The second clue lies in the pattern: if there are birds in the design it will be intended as decoration for the home; no pious man would kneel on a bird to pray!

Prayer rugs are popular among the town weavers of Mashad, Afghan and Balouch. Floral prayer-style rugs are often woven in Esfahan, Qum and Tabriz.

Another popular religious design, sometimes incorporated with the prayer arch on one rug, is the Tree of Life. This is an ancient symbol common to many religions, including the Christian faith. For the Muslims, living in lands where water is in short supply, the Tree of Life is a symbol of Paradise: the Koran promises the Faithful an eternal life passed in green and leafy gardens. It is also a symbolic representation of man himself, standing upright,

Tree of Life, Kashan, wool on cotton, early twentieth century, 6'5" × 4'7" (Ref. 1587)

This rug has a quality, style and palette which is often described in the international carpet trade as 'Mohtashem', a word which in Farsi means 'most noble' but was also the name of a very famous late nineteenth- early twentieth-century Kashan *ustad*, three of whose signed rugs are known. Stylistically, this amusing prayer rug falls into the 'Mohtashem' range and the very Sarouk-like floral border on a dark blue ground is also a characteristic of Mohtashem's known work.

rooted in the earth but growing towards heaven.

Once again, the design is common to both tribal and city rugs. In its simplest form, the tree comprises one straight vertical line representing the trunk, with a series of short horizontal lines for branches. In city rugs it is often highly elaborate and realistically drawn, sometimes placed in a garden of flowing streams and flowering plants where small animals and birds shelter. The towns of Esfahan, Qum and Tabriz are famous for their life-like tree patterns.

In some rugs, two trees stand side by side, with their branches entwined. These are woven to celebrate a wedding, and the significant inclusion of birds' nests in the branches can be interpreted without the need for scholarly research! The kind of tree is also symbolic: the weeping willow stands for sorrow and death,

Tree of Life, Esfahan, wool on silk, twentieth century, signed: Iran–Esfahan–Haggei, 6′2″ × 4′5″ (Ref. 1533)
Pictorial carpets of this kind are greatly favoured by Iranian connoisseurs of twentieth-century weaving although they have always been less in evidence in the West. This example has many design features derived from earlier Persian carpets and textiles and is an interesting example of its kind. The Tree of Life and butterflies, expressing life in Heaven, are extremely finely knotted.

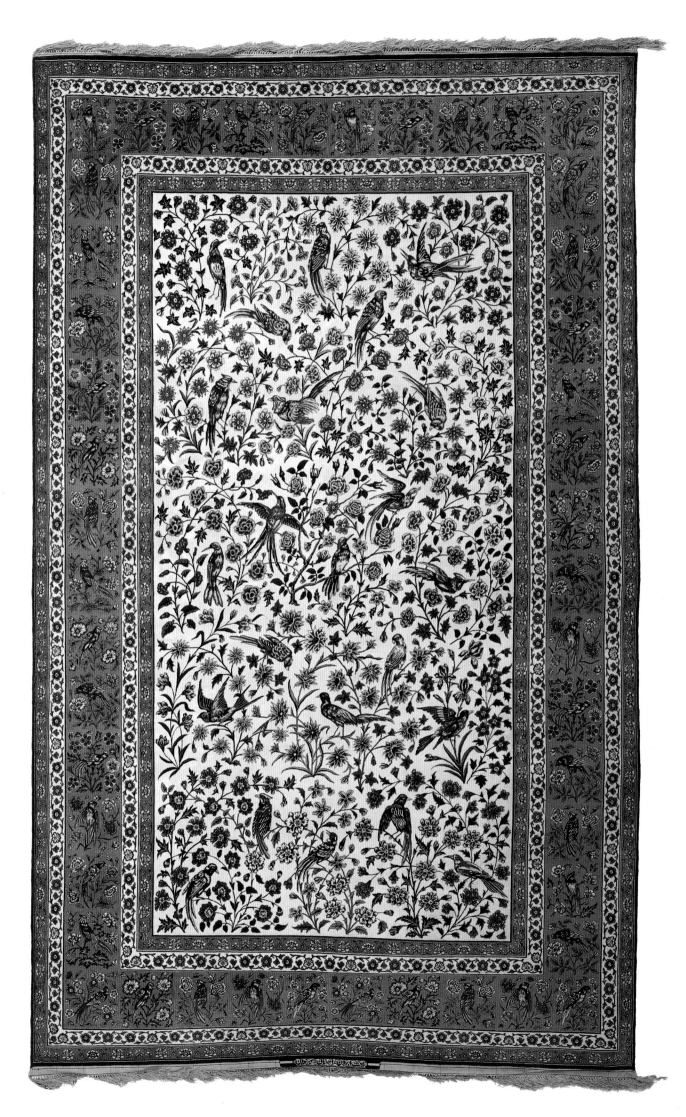

while the cypress indicates everlasting life.

The 'Vase of Immortality' design has similar symbolic significance, and it too is sometimes placed beneath the *mihrab* on a prayer rug. The vase is traditionally shaped like a Greek urn, filled with flowers. This design is popular with city weavers and can be very realistically interpreted, spreading to fill the whole field of the rug. A variation on this pattern is the 'Vase' carpet, in which small, flower-filled vases cover the entire field of a rug in a continuous interconnecting pattern.

The 'Medallion' design is apparently abstract in origin. Yet it too has great religious significance. The centre point of the medallion is said to represent the all-seeing eye of God. Some say its pattern is based on the lotus flower, which has always been regarded as a sacred symbol since it grows in the mud, but turns its wonderful blossom to the heavens. However, it is most likely that this design derives from the ceilings of the mosques. In the reign of Shah Abbas I, the finest decorators were chosen to create mosques of unrivalled beauty as a homage to God. It was they who decided that everything should match, and rugs be woven to mirror the ceilings (French weavers later adopted this idea when they wove for the great palaces). In some rugs a quarter of the central medallion is repeated in each corner, creating a harmoniously balanced design and a sense of continuity.

A variation on the basic pattern is the 'Tear Drop Medallion', in which the central, elongated sphere is finished at top and bottom with additional elipses, thought to symbolize God's tears. This

Opposite –
Sirafian gol-bol boul, Esfahan, wool on silk, mid-twentieth century, signed: Iran–Esfahan–Sirafian, 10'2" × 6'9" (Ref. Gol-bol boul)
This very finely knotted rug is a masterpiece from one of the greatest Persian *ustad* of the twentieth century and certainly the most active in the country since World War II. Iran is known as the land of flowers and nightingales, and the lovely design seen here incorporates both into a pattern known as 'the nightingale flower' (in Farsi *gol bolboul*). To Iranian connoisseurs, such a rug as this represents the very peak of contemporary weaving art. This piece certainly is one of the finest and rarest in quality made by the Sirafian family.

Medallion, Esfahan, wool on silk, mid-twentieth century, 7'9" × 4'10" (Ref. 1527)
This small rug illustrates late Pahlavi period Esfahan weaving at its finest. All of its individual motifs as well as the general composition are descended from Kashan and Esfahan rugs of the sixteenth and seventeenth centuries but are here rendered with the fluency and using the colours which made Esfahan weaving supreme in the decades following World War II. Most probably the work of the *ustad* Sirafian.

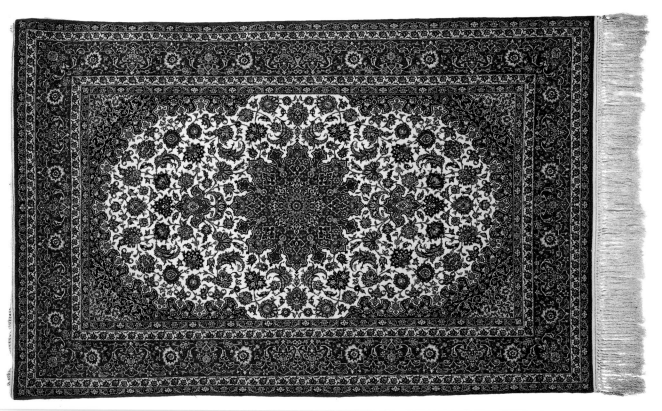

design first appeared during the Safavid dynasty of the sixteenth and seventeenth centuries, when court artists were encouraged to apply their skills to a number of different artistic forms. As a result this elegant design appears not only on carpets, but also on embossed leather book-covers, in particular the Koran. Western editions of the Islamic holy book habitually repeat the pattern.

Occasionally the weaver would sign his work, particularly if he was an acknowledged master of the craft. These signatures are usually placed on the upper short side of the rug in the middle of the lower border. If the script is on the upper edge of a picture rug it is usually the name of the person portrayed. If it is on the lower end, whether the design is abstract or pictorial, it is usually the name of the person who commissioned the piece. These 'rules of thumb', however, apply only to twentieth-century rugs from the major weaving cities. On older examples and on tribal pieces, the inscriptions almost always appear at the top, as is the case with all Bakhtiari rugs and carpets. On some rugs, including examples made in the sixteenth and seventeenth centuries, verses of poetry or, in the case of prayer rugs, inscriptions from the Koran, will appear in cartouches (decorative frames) all around the borders.

Historically, very few master weavers signed their work. Firstly, they didn't want their name to be placed on the floor and walked on! Secondly, such was their pride in the originality of their work that they felt it should be instantly recognizable without the need of a signature. This century, however, has seen an increase in the number of signed rugs, a change entirely due to the influence of the Western market. As weavers realized the importance of over-

Esfahan, wool on silk, twentieth century, signed: Iran–Esfahan–Akbaroff, 5'10" × 3'7" (Ref. 1531)
The interlocking stellar images both in the field and border date back in surviving Persian weaving to at least the fifteenth-century Timurid Period and can also be found on the weavings of other great Islamic cultures, for example the Moors of Spain and the Mughals of India. The composition is related to the tile decoration of mosques. The particular shade of royal blue used for the field of this rug is associated above all with Esfahan.

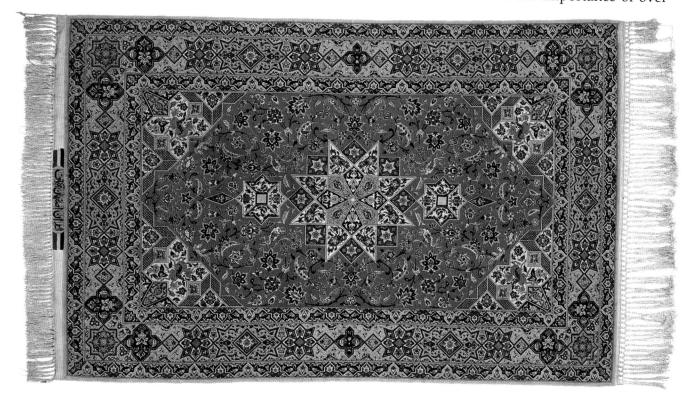

Gol farangi all over design, Karabagh, wool on wool, early twentieth century, 6'10" × 4'3" (Ref. 1376)
Yet another variant on the *gol farangi* pattern, although here there is another echo of the European origin of this design in the highly stylized and barely recognizable acanthus scrolls, depicted predominantly in brown, yellow and pink. There is an illegible inscription at the border of the carpet in an old type of writing.

seas buyers, they became keen that their names be known abroad. In addition, they were satisfying the Western buyers who were more attuned to painted works of art, where a signature was of paramount importance in deciding the value of a piece.

However, it is important to remember that, since any name can be woven into any rug, advice should be taken from an expert when buying a signed rug. Some carpet repairers will even weave a famous name into an existing rug, charging about £150 for the forgery. Therefore, a reputable dealer is of paramount importance if expensive mistakes are to be avoided. It should also be borne in mind that quality will show itself whether a piece is signed or not – a fine rug does not need a signature to be valuable.

Inscriptions are usually in Nastaliq script. This is an early form of Arabic writing, and its beautiful, flowing lines complement – and may even have influenced – the swirling arabesques which are so popular in city designs.

Verses from the Koran in cartouches are incorporated in many different designs according to the taste of the weaver. These appear

Tree of Life, Hereke, silk on silk, twentieth century, 3'5" × 2'7" (Ref. 1645)
Another splendid finely knotted Hereke of high quality, with over 1,200 knots per inch and a vine field border designed with peacock lovers. In the main field, birds sit on differently coloured trees; altogether a very charming rug.

either at the top of a one-way design, or placed within the borders. Occasionally weavers also included dates, poetry or a dedication to the individual for whom they were making the rug. While signatures and dates can add to the interest of a rug, it is unwise to attach too much significance to them. It is not unheard of for illiterate weavers to copy these details along with the design from a classical rug. It is also, of course, possible that the date is a fake to increase the price of a carpet – though any good dealer should spot the forgery, and would not risk his reputation by trying to fool his customers.

Religion has always been a very important part of life in Persia, and the teachings of the Koran have held sway. According to the Koran, no one but God can achieve perfection. In deference to this teaching, devout Muslims will sometimes include a deliberate mistake in their work, though it is not always easy to spot. It may only be that one tiny petal of a flower is coloured differently from the rest but the mistake, if you look hard enough, will often be there.

Particularly in the early Islamic days of carpet weaving the teachings of the Koran had a profound influence on the designs which could be woven. Since the Koran forbids any artistic repre-

All over design, Ravar Kerman, wool on cotton, late nineteenth – early twentieth century, 14'7" × 10'7" (Ref. 1443)
A quite unusual abstract field design from a region associated in particular with elaborate pictorial designs of the highest technical quality. The colour is particularly pleasing and the brilliant saffron main border is rarely encountered on Kerman weavings of this period. Ravar is a small village close to the city of Kerman where important weaving workshops were established in the second half of the last century; it is often misspelt as 'Laver' in Western literature.

sentation of living creatures, patterns were limited to stylized floral and abstract designs. However, such religious strictures tended not to be observed by the wealthy and powerful unless they were particularly devout, and many Imperial carpets from the Golden Age of the Safavid and Mughal Emperors in the sixteenth and seventeenth centuries have pictorial designs.

For example, the Shahs of the Safavid dynasty, in their pursuit of creative excellence, revoked this order, and the court carpets were suddenly alive with birds and animals. One of the most popular and enduring themes was the hunt. The importance of horses in a nomadic society is obvious, but for the Persians they are far more than beasts of burden. It was possibly the Persians who devized the game of Polo, and horses have always been among their foremost possessions. This has manifested itself in carpets in the 'Hunting' design, in which horsemen ride after wild animals brandishing spears.

The large numbers of prey depicted in these carpets are not merely due to artistic exaggeration. Historically, hunts were highly organized affairs, in preparation for which countless small animals were channeled down into narrow valleys which had been blocked at either end. In this way the hunters were all guaranteed a good catch! Hunting was far more than a pastime, it was considered the only sport worthy of kings. It was in the hunt that man exalted in his virility and skill, and displayed his power over animals.

Sometimes a rug shows animals fighting, usually a lion attacking its prey in an ancient symbol of good against evil. Some of the most striking animal carpets are tribal rugs depicting a single beast in a bold and abstract interpretation which rivals the most avant-garde of modern art. It is likely that all 'hunting' carpets, whether they show huntsmen as well as game or just the animals in a more

Samarkand, East Turkestan, wool on cotton, early twentieth century, 6'7" × 4'7" (Ref. 1554)
This delightful rug has a wonderfully comic tiger striding through a landscape. Rugs which simulate stretched tiger skins have become very popular of late, as indeed have all Far Eastern carpets with tiger designs. However, there is still a temptation to ascribe too many of them to centres in East Turkestan when it seems clear that the majority, especially such examples as this, were woven in Samarkand.

Medallion animal design, Qashqa'i, south-west Persia, Fars, early twentieth century, 8'5" × 4'11" (Ref. 1585)
This is another rug where the exact tribal origin is not certain – it is probably Qashqa'i but an attribution to the Khamseh or Luri is not impossible, especially as the weavers of these three groups borrowed designs from each other and all three used the distinctive blue and white 'block' pattern at each end. However, the main border design is typically Qashqa'i, as is the drawing, palette and the use of huge, stylized animals and birds both in the field and the medallions, all together making a very nice piece.

or less stylized floral setting, were intended as symbolic representations of Paradise, where, according to the Koran, such activities are promised to the Faithful.

The distinction between geometric tribal rugs and floral city rugs is clearly delineated. The same designs often co-exist in both communities, but vary in the way they are executed. As a more primitive people the tribal weavers produce simple, abstract interpretations in which traditional symbolism can be recognized without too much difficulty, since it is not hidden behind highly developed artistic conceits.

Since tribal rugs are woven without cartoons, they have less elaborately conceived designs when viewed as a whole, but make great use of individual elements to create wonderfully patterned rugs.

Their view of life is fatalistic, summed up by a line from Omar Khayam – "Tomorrow's tangle to the winds resign." Anything bad which happened was blamed on the Evil Eye, a malevolent force which could be kept at bay with charmed talismans. Blue beads, supposedly a powerful force against evil, were often sewn onto the edges of carpets. Some patterns were believed to have a similar effect.

The hardships of tribal life are often apparent in the motifs included in their carpets. A stylized dog may be worked into the pattern in the hope that this protector of the house will ward off thieves, illness and evil spirits. Similarly, an abstract representation of the tarantula is believed to keep the real thing at bay. Roosters, regarded by many tribes as the embodiment of evil, were believed

Gol-bol boul, Tabriz, wool and silk on silk, twentieth century, signed, 8'5" × 5'2" (Ref. 1360)

Since at least the fifteenth century, Tabriz has been one of the great weaving cities of Persia and was at the forefront of the great weaving revival which began about 130 years ago. This rug is most unusual and shows the hand of a distinctive artist. Its colouring is very vivid and the handling of the elaborate border design very assured. Tabriz rugs on silk foundation are very unusual.

to be powerful protectors.

Amongst the more positive symbols is the pomegranate, a many-seeded fruit which is a clear symbol of fertility. The inclusion of simple houses and gardens is a poignant reminder of the deep-rooted desire felt by many nomadic people to find a place to settle permanently.

There is a similar impulse towards the comforts of home behind the 'Persian Garden' design, of which the Spring Carpet of Chosroes is the earliest known example. Gardens have always been tremendously important to both village and town dwellers, living as they do in an arid and often inhospitable land. The writer E.C. Browne, on a visit to Persia in 1893, commented, "The Persians take the greatest delight in their gardens, and show more pride in exhibiting them to a stranger than in pointing out to him the finest building."

In such a dry country, irrigation was the gardeners' foremost concern, so they created rectangular gardens with grids of small streams between the flower beds. Garden carpets follow precisely the same plan. The walls of the garden become the borders, the streams are a grid across the field of the carpet – sometimes they even contain small fish. In the squares between lie plants, trees and animals, and occasionally a house. The Bakhtiari tribe, a nomadic people who could never own a real garden, are particularly fond of this design. They weave every square in a different background colour, creating a wonderful patchwork effect. This design is also popular with the weavers of Qum.

Tribal weavers work primarily to furnish their homes. Rugs are only sold when the family needs to raise money for a special occasion, maybe a wedding celebration or the birth of a child, and are therefore woven in patterns which appeal to the people who make them. This usually means that they are very bold and brightly coloured, and to the Western eye can appear brash.

Town and city weavers, who make rugs simply to sell in the bazaars, recognized this difference in artistic taste many years ago. As a result they modified the colours that they used to make their work more attractive to Western purchasers. Consequently, one town may produce two slightly different styles of carpet, one for sale in the East, the other for the Western market. One such example is the town of Kashan, which produces paler rugs, known as White Kashans, in which the background colours are creamy white, pale blue or green, rather than the strong colours which are traditional to their work. The patterns, however, are based on those which have been woven for centuries, and continue to delight the eye and enhance the home, whether in England or Iran.

Sarouk, wool on cotton, early twentieth century, 6'8" × 4'2" (Ref. 1536)
A splendid Sarouk with an elaborate floral arabesque repeat in the field. Both the design and the colours, as well as the particular rendition of the 'turtle' palmette border, are all distinctive characteristics of north-west Persian weaving and of Sarouk weaving in particular; they can be found in closely related versions on rugs from many different weaving centres influenced by Sarouk.

SETTING THE SCENE

The real beauty of oriental rugs, for many modern buyers, is their absolute originality. No two rugs are exactly alike, in just the same way that no two paintings, or even people, are identical. Visitors may admire your wall-to-wall Axminster, then go out and get the same for their home, but however hard they try to find an exact replica of the wonderful oriental carpet in your living room they will never succeed.

The range of styles and colours available is so great that, for once, you can be sure of finding exactly what you are looking for.

If you don't know what you want then this wide choice can seem like a handicap in itself. The best way to choose is simply to visit as many carpet shops as you can, establish how much you can spend and then look at as many rugs as you like. In fact, once you show an interest, it can be a problem getting out of a carpet shop. Do not be afraid of asking the salesman to stop if you feel you have seen enough, or that the rugs are getting out of your price range – rugs are heavy things and he will be only too pleased to save himself unnecessary effort.

Never be pressurized into buying the first rug that catches your eye – in fact, never be pressurized into buying at all. You will know when you find the right rug, and a good salesman will leave you to decide for yourself. He may even dissuade you from buying

Opposite –
Leaders of the World, Ravar Kerman, wool on wool, c.1900, signed in Farsi and French: Fabrique de Milani Kerman, 8'0" × 5'0" (Ref. Leaders)
This splendid and extremely finely woven rug uses a very distinctive design, known as 'The Leaders of the World'. At the top are Prophets from the Old Testament, including Moses, and in the centre, Christ. These 'portraits' range down to the bottom right, where we can see Napoleon. The identity of each person represented is given in border cartouches in both English and Farsi. Such rugs were obviously very highly regarded among wealthy Iranians.

Al over boteh design, Doroksh, wool on cotton, late nineteenth–early twentieth century, 10'7" × 5'7" (Ref. 1140)
This dramatic carpet from Doroksh has a tightly drawn and organized *boteh* repeat in the field, a pattern found on Persian carpets from all over the country from the nineteenth century onwards. The elegant main border design is worthy of special note. An unusual rug for its size and quality.

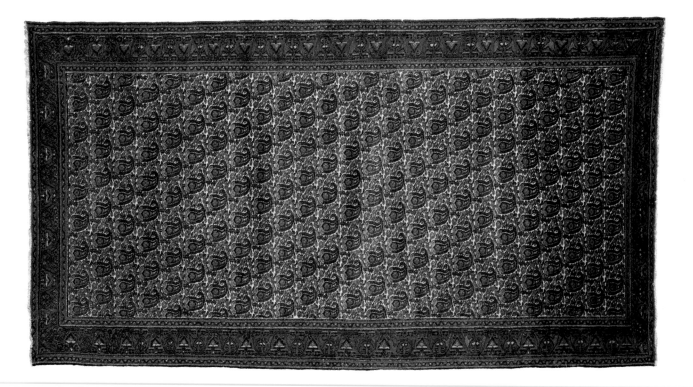

a rug until you have had a chance to look round other shops properly – which in our hard-selling society can come as a great, if welcome, shock.

Begin your selection process by making notes on every rug that appeals to you, jotting down colours, basic pattern and size. As the list grows you will begin to see certain common features: perhaps they are all geometric tribal rugs, or predominantly pastel in colour. Whatever the unifying features, it is important to consider these in relation to the room you are furnishing.

Look at the proportions of the room – is it high ceilinged? Is it a regular shape? Is there plenty of natural light or is it rather dark? Consider the character of the room as well – does it have any dominant features, maybe a large fireplace or an elaborately moulded ceiling? Whatever the main characteristics, you must then decide whether you want your rug to harmonize, or to contrast with them.

Generally speaking, richly patterned city rugs complement antique furniture and a period room, as do dark or pastel colours. Modern rooms often look best with bold, abstract tribal rugs in vivid colours. If furnishing an ultra-modern room, beware that your beautiful antique rug does not appear shabby in contrast.

When choosing a rug to blend in with the existing decor, it is important to establish the dominant colour of the room beforehand.

Medallion, Sarouk, wool on cotton, early twentieth century, 7'1" × 4'5" (Ref. 1546) Another tightly woven, beautifully coloured and delicately drawn Sarouk rug of high quality. The large medallion and shield-like pendants show a continuous design tradition from the Safavid era but in style and colour this rug shows great originality.

Qashqa'i, south-west Persia, Fars, wool on wool, early twentieth century, 8'10" × 5'1" (Ref. 1206)
This rug is typical both in design and colour of a well-known group of Fars weavings usually attributed to the Qashqa'i. Considerable argument rages over the significance of the motif seen repeated in the centre of each of the three conjoined medallions; many writers consider it to be a late and stylized rendition of what was once a Qashqa'i tribal emblem. Note the myriad bird, animal and stylized floral motifs filling the dark blue field around the medallions.

Working in natural daylight, look at the room through half-closed eyes. Since your vision is blurred, this allows you to pinpoint blocks of colour rather than specific objects. Note these down, then decide whether you want the rug to harmonize – for a traditional effect – or contrast – to give a more contemporary feel. Use this as a general guide, together with your check list of attractive carpets, to pick out a suitable example.

However, never buy a rug simply because it goes with your curtains. Curtains may last ten or fifteen years, but a well cared-for carpet will be with you for the rest of your life – so choose one which you like for itself.

Though design and colour are usually the primary considerations, it is also important to bear in mind how much wear the rug will have to withstand. If the rug is to be placed in the main entrance hall it is sensible to choose one woven in sturdy wool. However, do not be afraid to use silk carpets. Silk is beautiful, and actually very hard-wearing – after all, parachutes, as well as most museum carpets are made of silk! You should never be afraid of walking on a pure silk piece, although many people still prefer to lay them in a bedroom, where they do add an undeniable touch of luxury.

Size is another important consideration. We are used to wall-to-wall carpeting, and consequently many people make the mistake of buying a rug which is too large for their room. Rugs need to be framed in the same way that a painting does, and it is important to leave sufficient space round all four sides to set off the rich patterns.

If you are lucky enough to live in a large house, there are some exquisite large carpets to be found if you look around, though they

Overleaf left –
Moharamat, Tabriz, wool on silk, twentieth century, 13'0" × 9'9" (Ref. 133)
Another exceptionally finely woven carpet from Tabriz on silk foundations. Particularly interesting is the tension set up in the field between the vertical 'cane' pattern and the diagonally slanting floral arabesque 'waves' which overlay it. The pale blue of the main border is a surprising and pleasing element.
right –
All over design, Ravar Kerman, wool on cotton, late nineteenth century, 18'3" × 10'11" (Ref. 1559)
The design in the border of this carpet, not so much the cypress trees but the floral arrangement between them, immediately indicates this rug's origin. Both in colour and weave, it is typical of those associated with the products of factories established by the turn-of-the-century Governor of Kerman, the Farmanfarma. The field design and its use of floral motifs are reminiscent of eighteenth-century *mille-fleurs* carpets.

Vase design, Esfahan, wool and silk on silk, twentieth century, signed: Iran–Esfahan–Shah Hosseini, 5'10" × 4'0" (Ref. 655)

Another superb small Esfahan prayer rug signed by a well-known master weaver and in a most unusual palette. The use of bluish-purple and yellow in the rich and densely decorated field is most effective and the ivory ground cartouches with their floral decoration in the main border are most delightful. Silk has been used extensively to highlight the pile, as is often the case with the most luxurious Persian city weavings.

are more rare than conventional sizes. Should you later move and find the pieces do not fit into any of your new rooms, it is worth remembering that the owner of your old home may well wish to buy the carpets, and save himself the effort of finding more oriental rugs that suit the space.

There is one location, however, for which you must be certain that your chosen rug is large enough – the dining room. If the rug is intended to lie under a dining table it must be wide enough for chairs to be drawn back without catching on the edges. If not then it will be dangerous for the assembled diners, and will also be extremely bad for your rug. Repeated friction of this kind rapidly wears the side cords which hold the piece together, reducing the rug's value and life expectancy.

Luckily one of the many advantages of oriental rugs is that they are available in an enormous range of sizes. In the Persian language each size of rug has its own particular name. *Qalicheh* is the most common Persian word for rug, but in fact this denotes a piece of 7' × 4', or *dozar* size – a *zar* is a measure, and *dozar* means two *zars*. The smallest rug size is called a *pushti*, 3' × 2'. *Pushti* also means 'back', and *pushti* rugs are traditionally used to cover cushions which are laid against the walls for seated guests to lean against, but also as rugs to be laid in front of a door. The other common size is the *zaranim* – 5' × 3', or one and a half *zars*. Traditionally, until the nineteenth century, most rugs were *kelehs*, measuring 8'6" × 5'. These were used in the long rooms of Persian homes in an arrangement with *kenarehs* – literally, 'banks of the river' – which, as their name suggests, are long, thin rugs. Since European rooms tend to be almost square in plan, the Persian arrangement of one *keleh* at the head of the room, and a *kenareh* down either side does not really work. However, *kenarehs* are often of perfect proportions for corridors and narrow entrance halls.

Most tribal rugs, being made on small portable looms, are limited in size. However, this was not always the case and many very large Persian tribal rugs are known to exist, particularly those of the Khamseh of Fars and the Bakhtiari, as well as the great Central Asian Turkoman weaving tribes such as the Ersari Beshir and the Tekke.

As the city carpet weaving industry becomes increasingly commercialized, the range of sizes available is now almost infinite. Rugs can measure over 14' × 10', though clearly the larger a rug is, the more expensive it will be. If you want a particularly unusual shape, or a very large piece, these can always be arranged through specific commissions, though you may have to wait years for the work to be completed.

If you are planning to place furniture on a rug, there are several

All over herati design, Feragahan, wool on cotton, late nineteenth century, 18'8" × 10'10" (Ref. 42)

Huge numbers of such carpets in varying qualities and sizes were imported into Europe and the United States between about 1870 and 1930 through the more exclusive shops and can still be found on the floors of innumerable English country houses. They were strongly made and at their best, as here, were very hard-wearing – as they needed to be. The field design is usually referred to as the *herati* pattern after the Eastern city of Herat, once in Persia but since the early eighteenth century in Afghanistan, although there is no real reason for this. Notice the beautiful 'turtle palmette' border design and the attractive ivory ground corners which lighten the heaviness of the field.

points to bear in mind. A rug will not be damaged simply by having a weight placed upon it, though the pile can become compressed with time (so it is a good idea to move heavy furniture slightly from time to time). However, if anything sharp sticks into the rug it will become damaged, so unless the furniture legs are of smooth wood it is best to put castors between them and the rug.

The other consideration when positioning furniture is the effect it will have on the design of the rug. If a table is placed in the centre of a medallion rug it can lose much of its impact, since the main feature will be covered. A simple solution to this problem is to choose a glass table, which will protect the rug, and show off its beauty. Similarly a large piece of furniture obscuring one section of the rug can destroy any balance the design may have. If a rug is to be covered it is usually best to pick an all-over design. The other option, of course, is to move either the furniture or the rug.

As important as what goes on the rug is what goes underneath it. If the floor is uneven, the rug can wear in patches, considerably reducing its value. A well-padded backing strip helps in this situation, as does regular turning of the rug, which evens out the pattern of wear. Generally speaking, if there are any sharp protrusions, for example uneven flag-stones, it is probably unwise to lay a carpet there at all until the floor is evened out by a builder.

Polished floors of wood or stone provide a marvellous backdrop for oriental rugs, but it is important to use a good quality non-slip rubber underlay to prevent the rug skidding around. Many people now lay their rugs on top of existing wall-to-wall carpet, and this can provide the perfect backing. Patterned wall-to-wall carpets, however, are generally speaking not suitable, since they will almost inevitably clash with the design on the rug. Deep pile carpets also tend to be unsuitable, since they do not provide a firm backing, and rugs tend to creep and crinkle. If this happens,

Opposite –
All over herati, Doroksh, wool on cotton, late nineteenth century, 26'11" × 17'9" (Ref. 1630)
A vast and tightly woven Doroksh carpet from Khorasan. The dark blue field is covered with an elegant version of the *herati* pattern organized in such a way as to create parallel 'waves' down the entire length of the field, a masterly piece of design. The rich but subdued palette, with its emphasis on browns, blues and dark reds, is characteristic of late nineteenth-century Khorasani weaving.

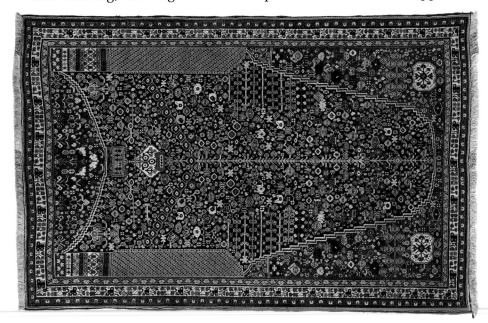

Mille-Fleurs, Qashqa'i, south-west Persia, Fars, wool on cotton, twentieth century, 8'0" × 5'2" (Ref. 1006)
Fars rugs in this distinctive design are usually ascribed to the Kashkuli tribe of the Qashqa'i Confederation and were almost certainly all woven in workshops rather than on semi-nomadic tribal looms. They are quite clearly based on a well-known but very rare group of eighteenth century Mughal prayer rugs, and known as *mille-fleurs* prayer rugs. The Mughal influence has never been properly explained but is thought to stem from the time of Nader Shah Afshar who sacked Delhi in the eighteenth century and who was based in Fars, whence he returned with large numbers of craftsmen. A very charming rug.

Mohtashem, medallion, Kashan, wool on cotton, late nineteenth century, 10'5" × 7'5" (Ref. 1615).
A Kashan of the type referred to as 'Mohtashem'. The soft but subtle colouring is typical of weavings of this type and class and one is again struck by the relationship to Sarouk rug designs. It is interesting, however, that the main border pattern, with its flowering branches, is based on a Safavid Persian border design of the seventeenth century.

contact your carpet dealer and he will be able to provide you with the correct backing. Your dealer will also be able to help if the carpet begins to curl at the edges. He will stitch leather or rubber strips to the reverse edges of the rug, encouraging them to lie flat.

The positioning of rugs in a large room is particularly important. Though a single large piece can be overpowering, several smaller ones may be used to great effect to enhance each other, or help 'divide' an open plan room. If you decide to try this effect it is important that the rugs harmonize, otherwise even the most

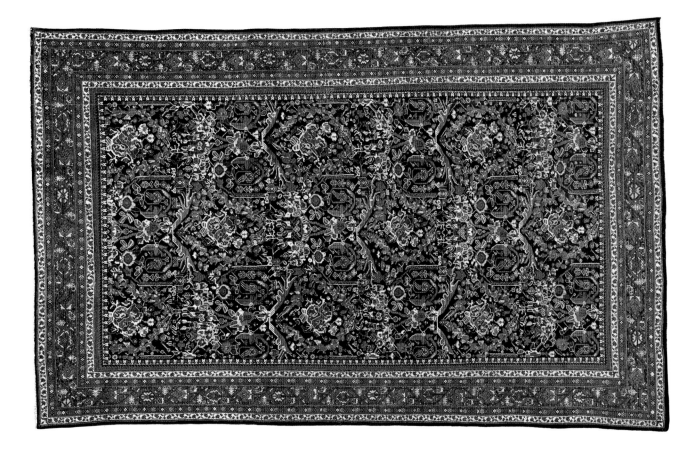

beautiful pieces will suffer. Apply the same sort of rules as you did when making your original choice – looking out for similar styles, colours and designs. Generally speaking, florals and tribals do not mix – though the 'Garden' design carpets from Qum, which are strictly speaking florals, can look wonderful with geometric tribal pieces. Tones should also be unified: in a combination of bright and muted rugs, the more vivid pieces may overpower the others. With colours the rules are less stringent, since most rugs contain a wide spectrum. As long as the rugs have at least one colour in common, and are of a similar tone, the combination should work admirably.

When combining rugs, the short-cut to success is to pick several rugs from the same region, since in this way you can be sure of picking pieces which have design and colour elements in common.

When considering the place a rug will occupy in your room, remember that the floor is not the only place it can be put. Rugs make superb and original wall hangings, and this can be a particularly good way to display a rug which is too fragile to withstand everyday wear and tear. Using rugs in this way is also a very economical alternative to buying a French or Belgian tapestry.

It is important, however, to hang the rug properly or the strain of supporting its own weight can damage it. One of the best ways to hang a rug is to sew a strip of cotton webbing to the upper side

Migon, wool on cotton, mid-twentieth century, 17′5″ × 10′6″ (Ref. 41)
A very attractive carpet with an elaborate floral design repeated in the field. Rugs of this composition are usually attributed to the Bijar area of north-west Iran.

Medallion, Hereke, silk on silk, twentieth century, signed: Ozebek, 9'3" × 6'9" (Ref. 1607)

The factory at Hereke in Turkey was established to produce cloth in the early nineteenth century but carpets were not woven there until 1891. They are among the most famous of modern carpets and the silk examples are especially highly prized. Some examples have been woven in recent years with spectacularly high knot counts, ranging up to an astonishing 2,500 or so per square inch! This rug is typical, richly coloured and based on Safavid Persian styles.

on the back using sturdy cotton thread and a large running stitch. A brass or wooden pole can then be inserted, and, supported by strong hooks, screwed into the wall and threaded through nicks in the webbing. This distributes the weight evenly along the length of the rug, preventing damaging straining and sagging. Almost any rug will make a fine wall hanging, but one-way designs and picture rugs are perhaps the best suited.

When it comes to placing oriental carpets, the possibilities are as limitless as your imagination. Small rugs, or pieces from badly worn larger rugs, make attractive cushion covers. They can also be used to upholster furniture, or cover tables – placed under glass if the table is used frequently. Remember that rugs are not the only woven pieces produced in Iran and the surrounding regions. Decorative strips, originally woven as hangings for nomadic tents, can be used as pelmets with curtains that pick out a dominant colour, or simply to frame a window. Saddle bags make excellent floor cushions, requiring nothing more than stuffing and stitching up on one side. People have even been known to use oriental carpet fragments on the floor of their car!

The search for the perfect carpet can be hard work, so it makes sense to look after it once you have found it. Rugs are basically quite resilient, though being made of wool they will not last forever – despite what you may have heard to the contrary.

The first rule of carpet care is to clean regularly. Dirt mars the beauty of your rug, and should be removed weekly using a vacuum cleaner or the good old-fashioned dustpan and brush. Work in the direction of the pile, avoiding the fringes. These fringes hold the carpet together and are threatened by repeated vacuuming, which may snap them off. Make it part of your routine to turn the fringes under the rug while you clean. Obviously, no one should embark on cleaning a rug without first having ascertained its condition; even light cleaning of a very fragile piece may cause further damage. If, however, the rug is in good condition, with no breaks or tears, beating the back with a hoover will remove any deeply impacted dirt; the piece can then be given a conventional hoovering on the front to remove surface dirt.

Every five or ten years, depending on the amount of traffic over the rug, it will need a thorough clean. This should always be left in the hands of a professional. It may seem extravagant, especially when there are so many books telling you how to wash rugs yourself, but if things go wrong (and they often do) the cost of replacing a rug will be far greater. Stories are occasionally heard about rugs which have been sent to the dry cleaners – and of course ruined in the process. It goes without saying that the only professional worth trusting is a skilled carpet cleaner. However, even a professional will not guarantee your carpet when cleaning it. Oriental rugs are hand-made, and therefore variable and unpredict-

Animal design, Karabagh, wool on wool, dated 1330 AH (1911/12 AD), 6'10" × 4'3" (Ref. 1609)
This delightful and most unusual rug has three rows of animals – horses, rams and dogs (which look like St. Bernards) – arranged on a plain crimson field. There are also two stylized floral motifs and a woven date which is wholly believable.

able. Minimize the risk involved by using someone recommended by your dealer.

Rugs should also be turned quite regularly to avoid the build-up of patches of uneven wear. Every year, rotate the carpet through 180° so that the main 'paths' across it are changed. Swapping rugs from room to room, if possible, will prolong their life for the same reasons – with the added bonus that, since most rugs are so versatile, the process can add a new lease of life to your decor. All rugs will fade eventually, even in weak British sunshine, though this obviously will take considerably longer than in brighter climates.

Since rugs are objects of everyday use, accidents will inevitably happen. If anything does get spilled on your rug it is important to act immediately to minimize damage.

The carpet's number one enemy is the household pet. Even a house-trained animal may have the occasional 'accident', and the acid present in urine can be extremely damaging. Not only does it

Vase design, Esfahan, wool and silk on silk, twentieth century, signed: Iran–Esfahan–Ramazan–Emadie, colours and design by Asgar Rasoulie, 5'7" × 4'0" (Ref. 688)

Emadie was one of the principal *ustad* of Esfahan and his work is particularly highly regarded by Iranian collectors. The colour scheme as well as the design of this rug is by the artist Asgar Rasoulie. The composition of a vast and dramatic spray of flowers emanating from an ornate vase was a favourite with Iranian weavers from the nineteenth century onwards and, as in this case, is often found on prayer rugs.

bleach dyes, but it may actually rot the base fibres. Blot up the excess liquid immedaitely with white paper towels until the patch is almost dry. Wash the area with the foam produced from a solution of two teaspoons of washing-up liquid or baby shampoo to half a gallon of cold water. Brush with a stiff bristled brush and allow to dry completely.

Other spilt liquids such as alcohol, tea and coffee, should be treated in much the same way. If food or mud is trodden into the rug, scrape off as much as possible without working it into the pile. The affected area should then be left until completely dry, when it is usually possible to brush away the remainder with a stiff brush.

The other great danger to rugs comes from moths. They love dark, undisturbed places, and the back of a carpet – whether on the floor or the wall – is a favourite location for them to lay their eggs. Heat kills these pests off, so putting your rugs out in strong sunshine from time to time can keep them at bay. There are also a number of moth-proofing treatments available, some of which are

Esfahan, wool on silk, twentieth century, signed: Iran–Esfahan–Reza Rezvani, 5'4" × 3'8" (Ref. 1037)

Another beautiful small rug based on the prayer rug format, although the *mihrab* or arch is implied rather than defined. It is interesting to compare this piece with the rug signed by the *ustad* Emadie (page 92). Both are clearly variations on the same design, which may have originated in eighteenth- or nineteenth-century European prints, probably of French origin. The two cornucopia and crossed pheasants at the top of this version are perhaps more pleasing than the variation on the Emadie rug but this is very much a subjective opinion; both rugs are outstanding and have extraordinarily subtle colours.

Tree of Life, 'Embossed' Kashan, silk and metal on silk, late nineteenth century, 6'9" × 4'3" (Ref. 1590)

Rugs in this particular technique are known universally in the carpet trade as 'embossed' or 'raised' silk Kashans. They follow a technique well-known from Safavid weavings, many of which were made in Kashan, and in particular a group of silk and metal thread pile weavings known as 'Polonaise' rugs made in seventeenth-century Esfahan. Here the flat-woven ground acts as a perfect foil for the brilliantly coloured piled silk flowers, the large palmettes being brocaded in their centres with silver-wrapped silk thread; the piled design, of course, is raised up in low relief, hence the names given to this particular group. Such rugs are very highly prized.

extremely effective. It is important, however, to read the instructions carefully to make sure that they do not contain any chemicals which might damage the rug. There is also one traditional remedy worth trying. Moths love feathers more than anything else. Presented with the choice between a bunch of feathers and a priceless oriental carpet to lay their eggs on, they will choose the feathers every time. Keeping a bowl of feathers in the room, and changing them regularly, can be remarkably effective.

If the moths have beaten you to it, or the rug has been damaged in some other way, there may be small areas in the rug where the pile has gone (the warp and weft threads are rarely affected since they are almost always made of cotton or silk). A timely repair will save a lot of money, and possibly even the rug itself.

Moths are not the only danger. Side cords are an essential part of the framework of a rug, but are subjected to the most wear and tear. As a result they need attention every ten years or so. In extreme cases the side cords can become completely detached from the main body of the rug. As already stated, the fringes are the other important area. If they become damaged in any way, or start to unknot, action should be taken immediately.

Whatever the problem, it is important that repairs are carried

out by a professional. On no account attempt to repair the rug yourself. A bad job may ruin a rug, and will certainly cost more to rectify than if it had been done properly in the first place. Beware of carpet repairers who quote very low rates. The small saving they offer could be completely lost if the work is badly done. Much less common, but more worrying, are the small number of so-called repairers, usually without a workshop of their own, who take a carpet to mend and then disappear, carpet and all! This may sound unlikely, but it has been known to happen. In the end, the safest option is to go back to the dealer from whom you bought the rug. He may have a repair workshop of his own, but if not he will certainly be able to put you in touch with someone reputable who does. Even so, it is important to get a receipt for the carpet when you hand it over, and to make sure that the repairer has sufficient insurance to cover the value of the carpet in case of accident. The repair may be more expensive than you expected, but will still be money well spent. There is an old Persian saying which sums it up perfectly, "I am not rich enough to afford the cheap option." A good quality repair will preserve, or even enhance the value of the rug, and will last for many years longer than a bungled job.

With proper care an oriental rug will continue to decorate your home for many years to come.

Mosque design (medallion), Nain, wool and silk on cotton, mid-twentieth century, signed: Iran–Nain–Habibian, 12'6" × 9'0" (Ref. 1592)

This is one of the greatest mosque dome designs by the greatest *ustad* of late Pahlavi period Nain weaving. The design itself, radiating straight lines overlapping to create a multiple diamond effect around a central medallion, can be traced in Islamic art to the ninth century and can be found used in the art of all Muslim countries in a variety of media. The dense drawing of this piece is remarkable and the carpet is very finely woven.

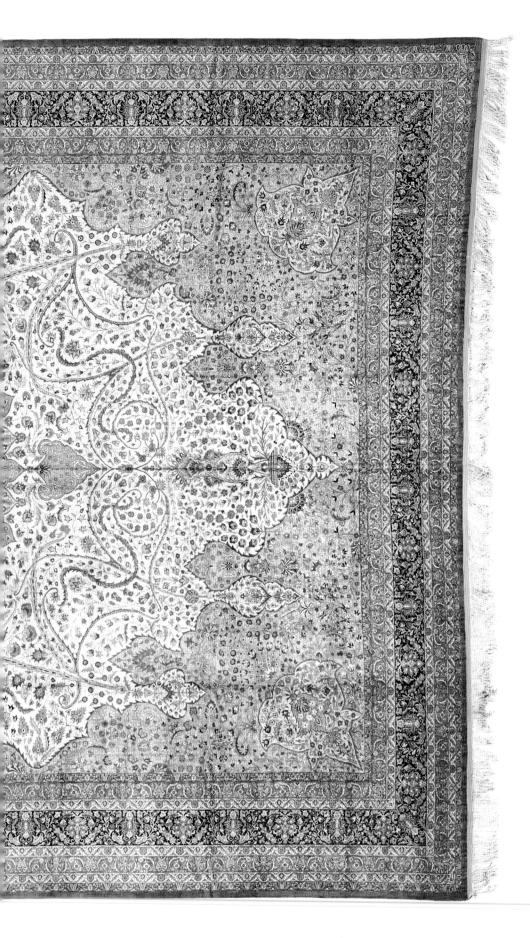

Turkish Kaiseri, silk on silk, twentieth century, 29′5″ × 20′4″ (Ref. 1622)

From the late nineteenth century onwards, a number of leading Turkish weaving centres, usually under Armenian direction, began producing carpets in Persian style pile either in silk or in wool, the latter often embellished with metal thread (the same phenomenon is often encountered in sixteenth and seventeenth century Persian rugs as well as ones of more recent vintage). Hereke and Kaiseri are the most famous centres of Turkish silk weaving today, although there are, and have been, many others. Turkish silks are renowned for their beauty of colour, elegance of drawing and, perhaps above all, fineness of knotting. All these features are present in this carpet but perhaps its most extraordinary aspect is its sheer size; few silk-piled rugs of these enormous dimensions have been woven in recent decades, either in Turkey or Persia.

CHAPTER SIX

THE SEARCH FOR TRUTH

With the question of design safely out of the way, the next consideration is to find a rug which represents good value for money. Clearly you want to find the best possible quality within your price range, but for many people this can prove to be the hardest part of the buying process.

Making an informed choice can be a daunting prospect for the novice, since to truly understand oriental rugs can take a lifetime. The connoisseur develops an instinctive feel for the subject during years of involvement, in much the same way as an expert in fine art does. The amateur cannot hope to compete, but with a little study can greatly improve the chances of making a satisfactory purchase.

In addition to reading widely on the subject, it is useful to visit a number of shops, noting style, size and price. In this way you can gradually build up a framework by which to judge other prices. When buying a new car you would not just go out and buy the first one you saw, but would compare prices and models. Certainly there are many more carpet 'models' around, and prices are less clear-cut, but the principle remains the same.

Since as a buyer one's knowledge is likely to be limited, it is

Opposite –

All over design, Tabriz, wool on cotton, late nineteenth century, 23'5" × 14'7" (Ref. 5661)
This splendid Tabriz carpet has a design and palette based on some magnificent seventeenth-century Safavid Persian carpets attributed to Esfahan and known as the 'strapwork' group. The 'strap-work' itself is a rendering of the 'split-palmette' arabesque or *rumi*, one of the great stylistic innovations of Islamic art; here continuous overlapping registers create a flowing geometric pattern over-laid by and overlying floral palmettes and leaves on a rich red ground.

Bakhtiari all over vase design, Chahar Mahall, wool on cotton, early twentieth century, 16'5" × 10'7" (Ref. 1561)
A very handsome carpet woven in one of the factories owned by the Great Khans of the Bakhtiari, in this case probably in the town of Shahr Kord. A design of flowers in coloured cartouches.

Malayer, wool on cotton, early twentieth century, 16'5" × 6'6" (Ref. 1601)
A quite unusual Malayer long rug with an elegantly drawn lobed medallion arranged on the diagonal axis in the dark blue field and containing another sytlized version of the *gol farangi* pattern. Another rug clearly influenced by Western taste and probably intended for the Western market.

All over herati design, Senneh, wool on cotton, first quarter of the twentieth century, 16'11" × 6'6" (Ref. 1625)
An extremely large and fine Senneh *kilim*, made with the *herati* pattern. *Kilims* of this type are usually 6' × 4', but this *kilim* is very rare indeed, for both its size and quality.

particularly important to trust your dealer. Avoid fly-by-night companies with short leases. Generally speaking also avoid shops with large, red 'Sale' signs in the window. Similarly, beware of any shops with 'Closing Down' signs, since this closing-down process has been known to take anything up to ten years!

Department stores, which generally stock carpets of only medium quality at best, are a different matter. These carpet departments are part of a large selling mechanism and may well have a limit on how long they can hold a particular piece. They may, therefore, reduce their profit margin to clear their stock room. However, just as you would not go to a department store to buy a fine painting, so you will not find a superb rug there. You may get a painting which is pleasant and adds colour to the walls. Equally, you may find an attractive floor covering, but it will be very different from the fine carpets you will find in a specialized shop.

Carpets in good condition rarely, if ever, lose value, however long they are stored, so such shops advertizing "50% off" are either

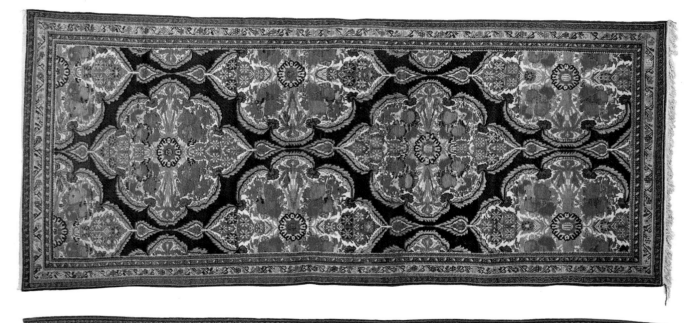

Medallion, Malayer, wool on cotton, early twentieth century, 6'6" × 4'8" (Ref. 660)

A lovely small example of Malayer weaving from north-west Persia of excellent quality and vivid colour. The all-over *boteh* vine design is typical, although it is interesting to note how it is used to such contrasting effect on the central ivory ground medallion as opposed to the dark blue field. Note the change in the mid-blue of the main border at the top, a tonal variation called *abrash*.

massively overcharging in the first place, or are having difficulty selling poor quality rugs. Good rugs will never be given a special sale price. The rug's value is calculated in terms of the materials it contains, the time it took to weave it and the quality of the finished product. In two years time all these factors will have increased in value, and hence so will the rug. It simply makes no sense to halve the price of a good rug.

It is possible that a dealer will sell a particular rug for something less than the price on the ticket. Perhaps he has been holding the rug for many years and needs to realize the value of some of his capital. Perhaps he hopes that if he offers the buyer a lower price for one rug then the customer will become a regular client. But one thing is certain – if a rug is good quality it will never be advertized in the window as being "at sale price."

Novices are best advized to steer clear of auctions. 'Country' auctions in village halls, special sales in hotel rooms and 'bankruptcy' sales near airports and ports are often used by disreputable dealers to off-load substandard rugs on an unsuspecting public. Even the large, established auction rooms can prove a minefield to the beginner. It is often difficult to look properly at the rugs beforehand, and once the bidding is underway it is all too easy to get carried away by the excitement and pay more than you would have done in a good shop. Remember, you do not know who you are bidding against – it could turn out that your rival bidder is in fact the carpet's owner, trying to push the price up. Auctions are a very good way of selling poor rugs; after all the owner has the protection of a reserve price so the piece will never be sold for less than its worth. Once the auctioneer's gavel has fallen you are committed to the purchase. In addition, you will not have the chance to try out the rug at home, or to exchange it at a later date should you want to.

In a good shop, if you buy a rug believing it to be a Persian and it later turns out to be a Pakistani copy, then you can return it and your money will be refunded.

The importance of a reputable dealer cannot be over-stressed. These men are usually Eastern themselves, and generally try to conduct their business honourably. Of course, they are in business to make money, but there is a big difference between a reasonable profit and an outrageous mark-up. A good dealer knows that people who buy one rug usually end up buying more, and a satisfied customer will keep coming back – and may even bring new customers with him. Consequently he will not risk his long-term reputation for a short-term gain.

Even if you read extensively on the subject of carpets there will be times when you need to ask advice. In fact, if the salesman is knowledgeable this can be an interesting and enjoyable way of building up your knowledge. To be sure that you are getting sound advice, notice whether he has to check the stock details to answer your questions about a particular piece. While he will probably need to look up the price, he should not need notes to talk about the origin, age and quality of a piece. If he does, then he knows little about carpets. Ask to continue your business with the manager, or go elsewhere.

Ahmad Medallion, Esfahan, wool on cotton, first half of the twentieth century, 6'11" × 4'7" (Ref. 1547)
Ustad Ahmad was certainly one of the most creative artists of the first half of this century, and although many rugs have been attributed to this artist, only the quality and colouring of this rug can testify that this is his work. Both in colour and style this rug is not typical of Esfahan weavings from the post-War period and probably dates from the 1920s or 30s. Its palette and the drawing of the floral sprays on the blue field owe much to Sarouk weaving.

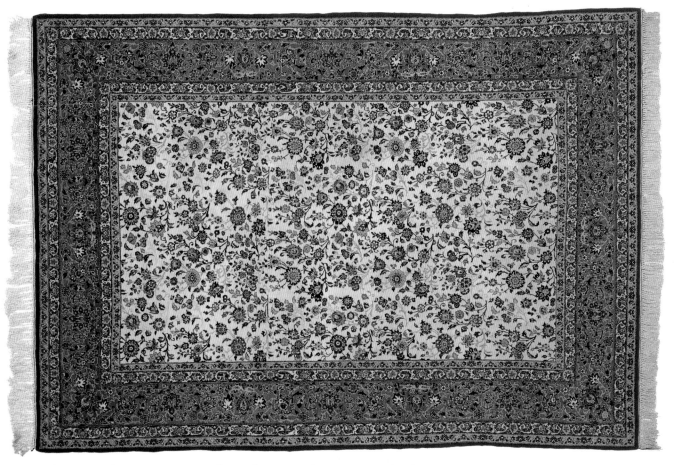

All over design, Nain, wool on silk, twentieth century, 7'5" × 5'6" (Ref. 1586) Almost all the Nain weavings illustrated in this book show the typical palette associated with rugs of this provenance. But in Persian weaving, things are not always as we expect; here we have a Nain rug with a much more robust palette closer in feeling to the Pahlavi period Esfahan rugs which had such great influence on Nain weavers.

There are, however, a number of points that you can look out for yourself. Most obviously, you should check that the rug in question is actually hand-made. Machine-made rugs do not wear well, lack the charming spontaneity of true orientals, and have no investment potential. So, though it may cost slightly less, a machine-made rug will never turn out to be the bargain you thought it was.

Luckily, machine-made rugs are easy to spot, even for the beginner. The basic test is to turn the rug over and look at the pattern on the back. If it is indistinct or invisible the rug is definitely machine-made. Hand-knotted rugs are made by tying each strand round the warp, so the colours are as clear on the back as they are on the front. In machine-made rugs the strands are not knotted at all, but looped and may be held in place with glue which obscures the pattern.

The other main danger to a first-time buyer is to be fooled into purchasing a reproduction rug. Many so-called Persians are in fact poor quality copies made in countries as diverse as Pakistan, China, Romania or Bulgaria. It is easy for the novice to be fooled, since the designs will be largely the same as the genuine article. An expert, however, will spot the forgery immediately and the rug will be almost worthless. Once again, safeguard yourself by choosing a dealer you have faith in, and make sure your newly acquired rug

Medallion, Sarouk, wool on cotton, early twentieth century, 12'0" × 8'9" (Ref. 1588)

If one had to imagine the most archetypal Sarouk medallion rug in the most characteristic palette, this would be it. The spiky floral fronds and branches on the dark blue ground around the central medallion are particularly distinctive, as is the red–ivory–blue radiation of the major field colours and the rust-red main border.

comes with a certificate of origin.

The next point to establish is the age of the rug. As a general rule, the older a rug, the more expensive it will be – providing it is in good condition – so it makes sense to check that it is the age a dealer claims. This can be quite tricky, and even experts cannot be very precise about the age of a piece.

When determining age it is not sufficient to go by the description on the sales ticket. The terminology used is often confused, and certainly confusing. The term 'antique' may be used to describe anything over 100 years old. 'Very old' means anything from 70 to 90 years; 'old' is over 55 years; 'semi-old' generally denotes a rug between 35 and 55 years. A 'new' rug can be anything up to 20 years old.

Age is highly valued in the carpet world because of the part which time plays in the enhancement of beauty. With use rugs acquire a distinctive patina, as the wool is gently polished by countless pairs of feet, and the colours mellow into rich, harmonious tones. A carpet which is shabby and threadbare should not be marked up in price simply because it is fifty years old. Rugs are objects of beauty, and when they lose their beauty they lose much of their value. The only exceptions to this rule are pieces which are many hundreds of years old, but these are unlikely to be placed on the open market anyway. Remember, an old rug is often worn, but not all worn rugs are old.

Also bear in mind that an old rug is not always more valuable than a new one. For example, fine quality newer (anything from the 1940s onward) pieces from Esfahan, Tabriz and Qum, and some new Turkish Herekes can be much more expensive than old rugs. Price, after all, depends on quality first and foremost. Age is not always the most important factor in deciding price. However, these remarks apply in the main to rugs woven within the last one hundred years. A surprising number of older examples, including masterpieces from the sixteenth and seventeenth centuries, still appear on the market and can often fetch enormous sums, as they deserve to. But even a rug of this venerable age need not necessarily be very valuable if it is a worn, badly damaged and ordinary example of a well-known type. No one should ever embark on the purchase of a Safavid carpet without seeking expert advice.

With antique pieces so highly prized, demand tends to outstrip supply. Not surprisingly, there are individuals keen to make a profit out of the situation. 'Antiquing' rugs is on the increase, and the methods used are many and various. New rugs may be laid out in the streets of the bazaars where animals, carts and people can pass over them, treading in dirt and wearing down the pile. Rugs may even be deliberately damaged and crudely repaired to simulate age. Colours are sometimes artificially aged by washing the rug in weak bleaching solution.

There are a few tests which you can carry out to validate the age of a rug. The knots on the back of a rug which has become worn through years of household use will be flattened and polished. If the rug is artificially worn the knots are usually unaffected, and the

Medallion, Qashqa'i, south-west Persia, Fars, wool on wool, early twentieth century, 6'1" × 4'5" (Ref. 1545)
This is an example of a very well-known and extremely highly regarded group of small medallion rugs attributed to the Qashqa'i Confederation and to the Kashkuli tribe in particular. The drawing of the elaborate *botehs* surrounding the central red medallion are characteristic of weavings by this particular Qashqa'i tribe and this piece has the colour arrangement found on the majority of examples of this design type.

yarn may still be quite fluffy on the reverse. 'Antique' washing of the colours of a rug, to simulate gradual mellowing, can also leave tell-tale signs behind. Turn the rug face-up and break open the pile. If the colours have been artificially faded there is often a mid-tone band of colour half-way down the tuft. In rugs which have faded through the years the colour deepens gradually towards the knot where it is harder for the sun to penetrate. Older rugs are inevitably quite dirty, as the faker knows only too well, but the dirt of ages. will be ground into the knots of the carpet, whereas 'cosmetic' dirt may well just lie on the surface. Woven dates, as we have said, are not always reliable. However, the type of rug can be used as a guide to age, since some weaving centres, and even some designs, are quite newly established. For example, the town of Qum only began producing rugs in the 1930s, so it follows therefore that no Qum carpet can be over sixty years old.

Beyond this basic check-list it is almost impossible for an amateur to guess the age of a rug with confidence. A good fake, after all, can even fool the experts. Generally speaking, if you like a rug and are not being asked to pay over the odds simply on the grounds of its age, it is best to forget the question of authenticity and enjoy the rug for itself.

Whatever the age of a rug it is important to establish that the

All over gol-bol boul, Esfahan, wool on silk, twentieth century, signed: Iran–Esfahan–Reza Rezvani, colours and design by Ashar Rasoli and Rasol Abbassi, 5′6″ × 3′8″ (Ref. 1035)

As befits a rug signed by a leading Esfahani *ustad* and designed by two known artists, this piece has a very distinctive look. Free-standing shrubs and flowers with birds on a plain ground have been part of the design language of Persian weaving for centuries, both on pile carpets and perhaps more importantly on silk textiles to which, in many ways, this rug is indebted. This free-standing shrub drawing is continued in the main border which, however, has the distinctive Esfahan brownish-pink ground. Notice the elegant rose meander in the minor guards, rendered richer by the dark-blue ground.

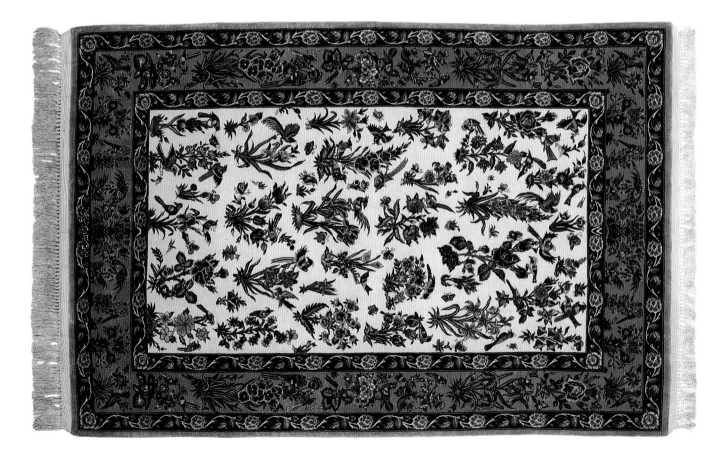

piece is in sound condition, otherwise your investment may simply unravel before your eyes. The biggest danger is from weak warp and weft threads, since these are the skeleton of the rug. They can be checked by folding the rug face inwards, and gently twisting with your hands. On no account use all your strength, since even the strongest rug may snap under the pressure – and never use this test on Bijars, which are so tightly packed that, however strong the base threads, they are threatened by the slightest strain. However, if you hear a slight cracking when you apply light force then the warp and weft are rotten, and the rug has little value. Mildew is another great enemy, but can be checked for by turning the rug face down and looking for tell-tale light patches.

Dirt is often the natural result of years of use, and can be removed by specialist cleaners. Heavy soiling, however, can conceal permanent stains which drastically reduce the value of a piece. If you are considering buying a very dirty rug, ask the dealer to have it cleaned first. If he is reluctant to do this, you should view the piece with suspicion.

Repairs are also an inevitable part of the ageing process. Good repairs can be hard to see, but they can usually be felt. To check for repairs slide your hand over the front and back of the rug, feeling for irregularities and bumps. Sometimes these may be due to uneven clipping, but generally they are the result of repairs. One or two small, well-executed repairs will not affect the value of a rug by

Medallion, Nain, wool and silk on cotton, twentieth century, signed: Nain–Habibian, 11'4" × 7'11" (Ref. 1552)
Another rug by the greatest *ustad* of late twentieth-century Nain carpets, Habibian. Although the palette remains typical, the extraordinarily elegant drawing of this piece and its great spaciousness marks it as out of the ordinary. The pheasants flying between the marvellous floral scrolls on the cream field, as well as the large palmettes, are all descendants of the Chinese style which had such great effect on Safavid Persian weaving during the sixteenth and seventeenth centuries and here retain an undimmed freshness.

All over Zelel-Soltan, Esfahan, wool on silk, mid-twentieth century, signed: Iran–Esfahan–Ahmad Zajaji, 6'11" × 4'5" (Ref. 1544)

Although not one of the best known *ustads*, this rug from the workshop of the master weaver Ahmad Zajaji is very beautiful and a highly original example of Pahlavi period Esfahan weaving. The all-over field pattern, with its delicate colour and repeated 'flower and vase' design, is possibly derived from the well-known rugs woven in the west Persian town of Abadeh.

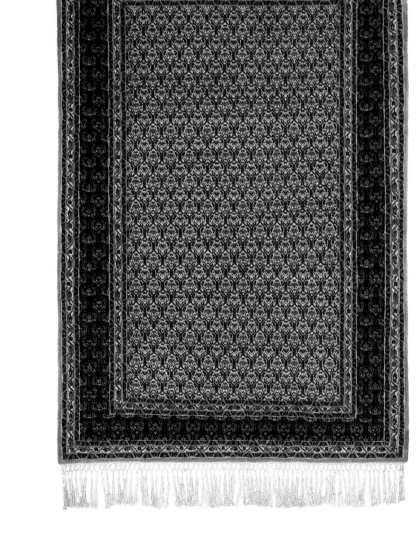

All over design known as 'Alaie', Esfahan, wool on silk, twentieth century, 5'2" × 3'6" (Ref. 1010)

A small rug with a most unusual, dense all-over field pattern, apparently a highly elegant major city workshop interpretation of a more rural rug weaving style. It is interesting how the design of the field is followed in the main border but to markedly different effect because of the change in ground colours.

much. If the repairs are crude, or there are more than two or three, the price begins to suffer.

As important as actual repairs are those areas in need of repair. Check for holes by asking for the rug to be held up to the light. Looking very carefully you should be able to spot even the smallest of faults. Do not be surprised or disappointed if you find one or two. The dealer should happily repair these for you free of charge, and as with existing repairs they will not affect the value of the rug if well done.

Once you have tested to the best of your ability that a rug is in good condition, you should check that the rug is complete. This is not as ridiculous as it sounds. If a piece is badly stained or worn around the edges it is occasionally trimmed down to remove the damaged areas. Sometimes this results in a strangely unbalanced design, which significantly reduces the value of the rug. You should not even consider a trimmed rug unless the borders still run round the entire outer edge. Once again though, carpets are personal things, so if you like the piece, and feel the price is fair, then buy it – and save yourself some money!

There are many hundreds of different rugs woven in Persia alone, and it would be meaningless to judge all of them by the same rules. Rugs should be compared with others of the same type if the conclusions are to have any value. Rugs are named after the city, town or tribe where they were woven. Having said that, it is important to remember that the rugs from a certain city are not all produced by the same weaver. Since quality is the main factor in determining the price, the skill of the individual weaver is the most important thing.

Buying a rug is like buying gold. Nine carat gold and eighteen carat gold will have different prices, even though they are both 'gold'. Equally, if you see a 6′ × 9′ rug from Nain priced at £2,000 and next week see another one being sold for £1,800, it does not

All over design, Yomut, central Asia, wool on wool, early twentieth century, 10′10″ × 6′8″ (Ref. 1598)
This so-called 'main' carpet is by another of the great central Asian weaving tribes, the Yomut. On its characteristically aubergine ground are arranged elaborate medallions on the diagonal axis; these are known to Turkoman weaving specialists as *kepse güls*, and are usually found only on Yomut main carpets but occasionally on smaller weavings by the same tribe. The use of colour in the *güls* indicates that this is a twentieth-century weaving.

Medallion design, Nain, silk and wool on cotton, twentieth century, 14'6" × 10'3" (Ref. 1110)

The city of Nain, not previously known for carpets, became one of the principal weaving centres of Iran during the period of Muhammad Reza Shah Pahlavi, whose reign ended with the Islamic Revolution of 1979. Nain carpets are instantly recognizable by their palette, in which beige, blue and ivory predominate. Stylistically, they owe much to Esfahan weaving but nevertheless have a distinct aesthetic of their own.

mean that the price is coming down. The most likely reason is that the first rug was of finer quality.

Knot count is often regarded as the first indication of quality. However, typical knot counts vary from region to region, and it would be pointless to dismiss a tribal Qashqa'i rug, simply because it had a lower knot count than a piece from Esfahan, where rugs are renowned for their fineness. What is important is that the rug is a good example of its type. Generally speaking, the knot count of a tribal rug is not relevant to its price, though knot count would be a factor in the price of city and town rugs.

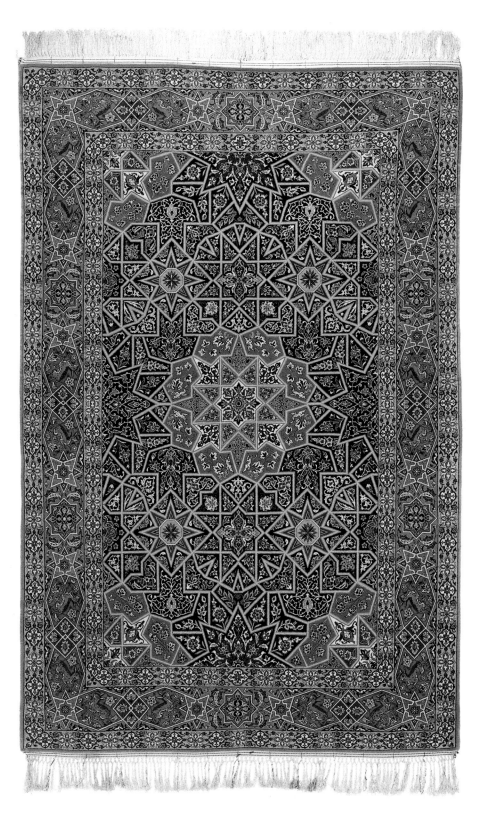

Medallion, Esfahan, wool on silk, mid-twentieth century, 7'7" × 4'11" (Ref. 1646)

A geometric medallion design, a very fine example of the Pahlavi period, probably the work and style of the *ustad* Hagigie. It is worth noting that the pattern of this rug resembles the design sometimes found on the Koran.

Similarly, the kind of wool is often highlighted, and a rug may be dismissed because its pile is not lustrous in comparison to another. However, once again, regional differences are the important factor. Most rugs are woven using local wool, and this varies in quality from region to region depending on the climate. The wool from Shiraz and Mashad is typically soft and lustrous, so it is

important to the quality of a rug from these regions that the wool displays these qualities. However, in Nain and Esfahan the wool is characteristically dry in appearance. A rug from Esfahan should not be marked down because it is without lustre, it should be judged instead on the tightness of its weave.

Clearly, if you are to judge a rug fairly, it is important to know where it comes from. This is not always as easy as it sounds. Spelling is not standardized, and there may be a number of variations on a single place name. In addition, the name on the ticket may not be that of the place it was woven, but the town bazaar in which it was sold. Also, not all words indicate place. There are various words used to describe size – *pushti*, *zaranim*, *dozar* and so on – which can confuse the amateur. There are also descriptive words, meant to explain more about the rug. *Kurk* is the name of a particularly high quality wool, either imported or grown domestically, and so may be included in the name to explain the higher price. This should not be confused with the word *kaba*, which is often used in the trade to mean 'coarse'. Other words help place the age of a piece – for example, a Taba-Tabriz is a modern day variety of Tabriz rug (Tabriz being the name of the capital city of Azerbaijan, in north-west Persia). Once again, the importance of a reliable dealer becomes clear. However much research you do, it

Opposite –
Esfahan, wool on silk, mid-twentieth century, signed: Iran–Esfahan–Sadeghe–Sirafian, 4′9″ × 3′3″ (Ref. 1624)
Another finely knotted rug from the great Esfahani workshop established by Sirafian after World War II. Although not unknown, pictorial or, in this instance, landscape carpets form the minority among Sirafian's work. Given the difficulties of the medium, one cannot help but admire this rug's remarkable technical achievements.

Medallion gol farangi, Karabagh, wool on wool, dated 1313 AH (1895/6 AD), 6′11″ × 4′7″ (Ref. 1540)
Although one should be a bit wary of dates woven into rugs, this one is entirely consistent with the piece's excellent quality and undoubted age. The off-set arrangement of large medallions on a blue ground is a little unusual and the rendering of the *gol farangi* pattern within these medallions is both original and charming.

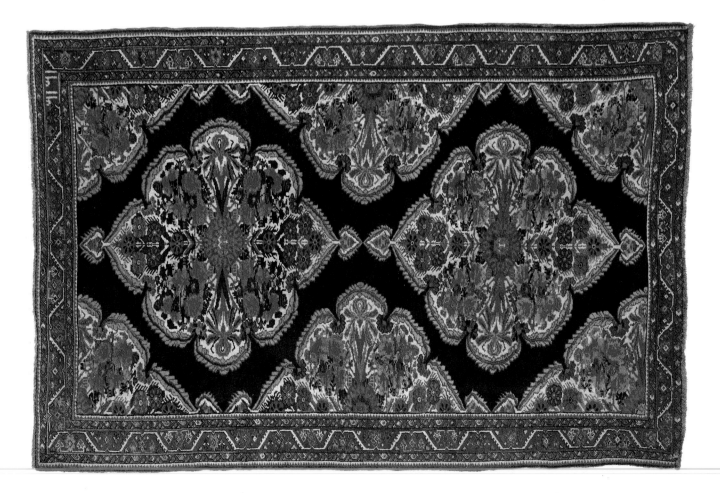

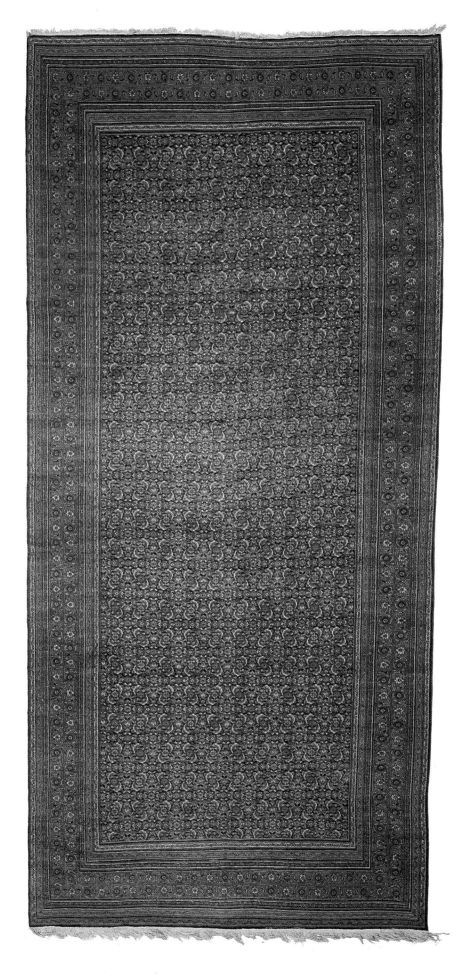

All over herati design, Doroksh, wool on cotton, late nineteenth century, 15'0" × 7'0" (Ref. 369)
This is a very interesting carpet using the *herati* pattern as the field design, the field being divided into implied vertical bands. This is an example of the brilliance and inventiveness of Persian weavers.

is likely you will need help at some stage in deciphering the sales ticket.

One final point to remember is that thick pile does not mean high quality. This is a popular misconception in the West, and has led to some kinds of rug being left with a longer pile than is traditional – these are often called 'American'. The Persians take the opposite view, as illustrated by the old saying, "The thinner the carpet, the richer the man." In fact, as with all features in a rug, what is important is that the length of pile is characteristic of the type of rug.

Medallion within a plain field, Doroksh, wool on cotton, late nineteenth century, 22'0" × 16'8" (Ref. 1571)

An unusually large and extremely handsome carpet from Doroksh in Khorasan. As is often the case with carpets associated with this location, the medallion and corners are placed upon a huge expanse of plain field; here they are richly dyed and woven from the most lustrous wool with a magnificent indigo background and extremely rare multiple borders.

Medallion, Nain, wool and silk on cotton, mid-twentieth century, signed: Iran-Nain-Jahangir Ali Mahri, 16'4" × 10'3" (Ref. 1498)

Another Nain typical in style and palette but of good quality and bearing the name of the *ustad* from whose workshop it came. Such signatures, although not necessarily indications of exceptional quality, were obviously reserved for the most part for carpets which the workshop in question felt proud to acknowledge. This example dates from the reign of Muhammad Reza Shah Pahlavi and was probably made in the 1960s or 1970s.

Medallion, Esfahan, wool and silk on silk, twentieth century, signed: Iran–Esfahan–Zolfagari, 10'7" × 7'0" (Ref. 626)

At first sight, the colour of this rug seems closer to that we have come to expect of Nain weavings than of those from Esfahan; but there is enormous subtlety in the use of colour here and both the drawing and the enormously complex central medallion, with its brilliant interior drawing, are typical of the work associated with the best Esfahani *ustads*.

Benaham Medallion, Tabriz, silk and wool on silk, twentieth century, 8'6" × 5'5" (Ref. 1506)

Looking at the complex and brilliant design of this rug, especially the radiating central medallion with its yellow and pink interior, it is not difficult to understand why many writers have suggested that here we have the symbolism of the cosmos, with the central medallion being the 'sky door', the entrance to heaven. Although such theories are often dismissed as fanciful, they are perhaps worth giving some credence to. The colour of this rug is of exceptional quality throughout, as is the weave.

116

Medallion, Tabriz, wool and silk on silk, twentieth century, inscribed (twice): *Farmayesh Parviz Fajian 1368* (Order of Parviz Farijan)', 10'0" × 6'9" (Ref. 1459)
A beautifully made carpet, unusual for a Tabriz in being on silk foundations, which was ordered by an obviously wealthy local dignitary. The colour is quite remarkable, as are the strange yellow panels with their inscription cartouches flanked by running hares.

Bakhtiari medallion, Chahar Mahall, wool on cotton, twentieth century, 10'0" × 6'9" (Ref. 1576)
A very distinctive Chahar Mahall design type known in the trade as *gol Ashrafi*. Particularly impressive is the dense arrangement of flower heads in the field around the huge central ivory ground medallion.

Bakhtiari all over medallion design, Chahar Mahall, wool on cotton, early twentieth century, 14'11" × 8'6" (Ref. 1602)
A typically lavish rug from the Bakhtiari-owned workshops in the Chahar Mahall Valley. The multiple star-medallion arrangement in the field is particularly attractive, as is the elegant floral border on an ivory ground, the latter probably derived from Esfahan city rugs. There is no evidence of the use of synthetic dye in this rug although it may well date from the 1920s or even the 1930s.

CHAPTER SEVEN

UNTOLD RICHES

sk anyone who has grown to love their oriental rug how valuable it is, and the chances are they will term it priceless. Like any other work of art, a rug can be valued in two categories – as a cherished object which has become part of the home, or as an item of investment. Also like other forms of art, the two are often hard to separate.

A price, of course, must be fixed if any object is to be offered for sale. In calculating a reasonable sum, the seller will take into account the cost of raw materials, labour and an acceptable profit margin. The level at which these sums are set depends to a great extent on two factors: cultural traditions and the cost of living.

Historically, nomadic weavers found it difficult to price their wares. The wool came from their own sheep and it was dyed by a member of the family using plants gathered from around the camp. The idea that a weaver's time might be worth something was a largely alien concept. Therefore, money did not enter the equation until the time came to sell a rug which might have taken years to produce. As a result the final price was often ridiculously low by any Western standard of market value.

City rugs, woven in factories where the workers are paid weekly and pre-dyed wool is bought as required, have tended to be more realistically priced – but only if judged in comparison with the tribal industry.

The concept of time as a marketable commodity has never been particularly strong in Iran. Had this not been the case, it is

Opposite –
Mohtashem medallion, Kashan, wool on cotton, late nineteenth century, 9′6″ × 7′8″ (Ref. 1616)
This carpet is of superlative quality and is of the kind which is often described in the international carpet trade as a 'Mohtashem' Kashan. It is interesting to note how the colour and, in some instances, the decorative elements, especially the main border, seem clearly influenced by Sarouk weaving. Fine Kashans of this kind are extremely highly regarded.

Medallion, Malayer, wool on cotton, early twentieth century, 12′2″ × 5′6″ (Ref. 1593)
A very unusual yellow ground carpet. Rugs of this colour are comparatively rare, especially from Malayer, and seem to have been very highly prized by Persian connoisseurs. The flowing, curvilinear style of drawing in the field is also unusual for Malayer weaving, although the 'turtle' palmette border is quite typical.

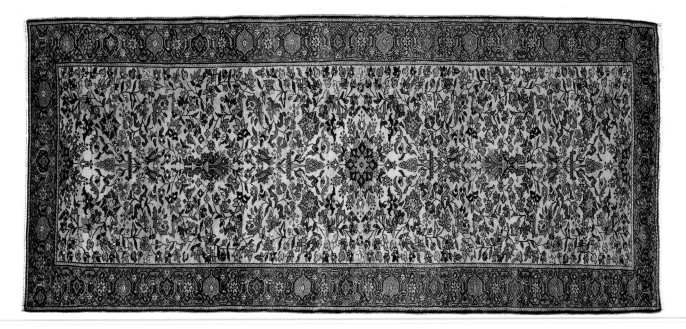

Bakhtiari all over design, Chahar Mahall, wool on cotton, mid-twentieth century, 10'3″ × 5'2″ (Ref. 1099)
This is one of the most famous patterns associated with the Bakhtiari and the workshops of the Chahar Mahall Valley. The best examples, of which this is one, were probably made in the town of Shar Kord. The alternation of the cypress tree with *gol farangi* bouquets in a lobed ogival lattice is characteristic of this design and the colour is also typical. A most unusual feature, however, is the simple border design with its tribal look.

Boteh all over design, Qashqa'i, south-west Persia, Fars, wool on wool, early twentieth century, 5'10″ × 3'5″ (Ref. 674)
Although stylistically unusual, the distinctive ends of this rug, with their blue rectangles set on white, indicate that this is the work of one of the great Fars tribal groups, in this case the Qashqa'i Confederation. The stencil-like drawing of the highly stylized floral motifs arranged diagonally on the dark-blue field indicates that the weaver of this rug may have been influenced by the rugs of the neighbouring Afshar tribe.

unlikely that the slow and painstaking work of the weavers would have continued until the present day. Their reward in the past has tended to be the satisfaction which comes from creating a beautiful object, rather than any financial consideration.

Since many weavers work from home their weekly 'wage' is actually rather difficult to calculate. However, to get an idea of the sum involved, take the example of a standard 6' × 9' Persian rug which takes one weaver about a year and a half to produce. The current market price for such a piece is approximately £1,100. A simple equation suggests that the weaver therefore receives less than £14 for his six-day working-week. However, the actual sum is even less, since this retail price includes all the interim costs of packing, transportation and wholesale and retail profits. If that same weaver were to demand an average European weekly wage of about £180, the price of this same rug would rocket to over £13,000. Take as a more meaningful comparison the example of a skilled carpet repairer working in Europe, who currently charges an average weekly rate of £300.

Only six in one million of the world's population are weavers. Of these, about one in three will be Persian and Turkish, the rest being Indian, Chinese, Romanian and Russian, to give but a few examples. Of the Persian and Turkish weavers, only one in five

could be called master weavers. Their work is highly skilled and the returns, as we have seen, are small. Obviously a direct comparison between the wages of an Iranian weaver and a European worker are not particularly meaningful, since the real value of a wage depends on the cost of living.

In the past the cost of living in Iran has been quite low. This is the only reason that weavers have managed to survive on their meagre wages. They have never, however, been well off. They live by and large in poor areas or nomadic tent communities. They exist without any of the luxuries which we in the West regard as an essential part of civilized living. Running water and electricity are largely unheard of. These people live at subsistence level. They grow their own food, take meat, milk and wool from their herds and have few possessions except those necessary for day-to-day life.

In recent times their condition has been exacerbated by the

Turkish carpet of 'Serapi' design, wool on cotton, first quarter twentieth century, 14'6" × 11'3" (Ref. 1562)
This rug is included to show how the carpet weaving styles of the Heriz area of north-west Persia were copied in other countries. Stylistically, it is quite typical but both its colour and structure are anomalous.

unstable political climate in Iran, which has led to spiralling inflation, a devaluation in currency, and a consequent dramatic increase in the cost of living.

The main currency units in Iran are the toman and the rial (10 rial = 1 toman). During the last Shah's time 11 toman were roughly equivalent to £1 sterling; a pint of milk cost two rial. Now there are 250 toman to the pound, and a pint of milk costs 25 toman. Clearly if the population is to survive wages must rise significantly – as they have been doing, day by day, even hour by hour.

Weavers, still amongst the lowest paid of all Iranian workers, have also seen an increase in their salaries in response to inflation. Since it may take many years for a rug to travel from the weaver's loom to the Western market, the inevitable effect on prices has not yet filtered through – but it is only a matter of time before carpet prices are forced to rise sharply.

Opposite –
Medallion, Mashad, wool on cotton, mid-twentieth century, signed: Shish-ghalani, 12′4″ × 9′8″ (Ref. 1454)
The signature of the *ustad* appears in a small cartouche in the centre of the top white ground guard border. This ornate medallion carpet is typical of the Mashad style developed by the great master-weavers. Most of their carpets bear a silk *kilim* strip on each side. Thanks to the patronage of Reza Shah Pahlavi, Mashad became the centre of carpet weaving before World War II. This colourful carpet is a fine sample of the style and design of that period.

Medallion, Tehran, wool on cotton, early twentieth century, 12′8″ × 9′9″ (Ref. 132)
Tehran, created the capital of Iran by the Qajars in the late eighteenth century, does not seem to have established a name for itself as a carpet weaving cen-tre until the first decades of the present century. Tehran carpets are usually of very fine quality. This example has a wonderful and dense flower and medal-lion design displaying superb work-manship. It seems reasonable to date it to the period before World War II.

Gol farangi all over design, Senneh, kilim, weft faced slit-tapestry on silk warps, twentieth century, 6'10" × 4'5" (Ref. 1610)

Senneh *kilims* are among the most highly regarded Persian weavings of the last two hundred years. The pattern is produced by the horizontal wefts and added fineness is given to this example by the rare use of silk warps (although all-silk Senneh *kilims* are also known). A very elegant version of the *gol farangi* pattern fills the field; note the charming and beautifully coloured borders.

The problem is exacerbated by the number of weavers leaving their traditional profession. As the war-torn country begins to take stock, shattered cities are gradually being rebuilt. Consequently there has been an increase in the demand for builders, and good wages are offered to lure people into the trade. For many struggling weavers the prospect of a decent salary has been sufficient to make them abandon their traditional work and move to the cities.

It requires only the most basic grasp of the laws of supply and demand to see that this factor will also force the price of carpets up. In the future fewer carpets will be produced, and those that are will be considerably more expensive – and probably many will be of a lower quality, as weavers speed up their work to maximize output in an effort to meet demand.

This demand comes not just from the West, where oriental rugs are now highly thought of, but from oil-rich Iranians and Arabs who are buying up high quality rugs as an investment, to protect their savings from the rapid devaluation of hard currency.

Rugs in the West are currently seriously undervalued, since the economic factors take time to filter through. However, the next few years will inevitably see prices beginning to spiral. Buying now not only virtually guarantees a sound investment, it may well be the last chance for all but the very rich to own a genuine hand-made oriental piece. A very fine Persian rug now costs something in the region of £10,000; in five years time its likely value will be in excess of £30,000. These figures are not mere speculation, they are a realistic forecast based on sound facts.

Even at today's prices, oriental rugs are the most undervalued of all art forms – and the fact that they are works of art cannot be questioned. In fact, it would cost more to commission an artist to paint a rug than it would cost to buy the rug itself.

Those who wish to invest in art generally think in terms of paintings, antique furniture, fine china and silver. Carpets, perhaps because they are walked on, are usually forgotten. When a painting is sold there is an exhibition, people gather and discuss the artist, his influences and his work. Carpets are never afforded the same treatment. If they were, however, those attending the exhibition would rapidly realize that a carpet is just as complex and interesting an art form as any painting. To really understand a carpet, it is

Medallion gol farangi, Karabagh, wool on wool, early twentieth century, 6'11" × 4'2" (Ref. 573)
Another typical 'Persian Karabagh' in the *gol farangi* pattern, although it has taken on something of the angularity of drawing associated with neighbouring Caucasian weaving.

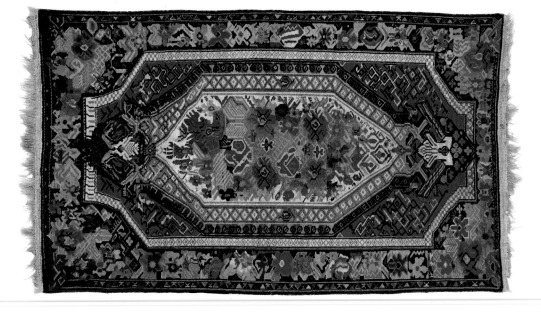

necessary to know something of the weaver, to know why he chose certain designs and colours, even why he was weaving it. The artistic value of a carpet goes far beyond the labour, wool and silk that went into its making, just as the value of a painting cannot be measured in terms of the paint and canvas it comprises.

Much respect is accorded to fine artists, but weavers have for centuries been almost forgotten. In the sixties, the Shah of Iran did begin to honour the great weavers of his country with gold medals for excellence. As a result fine weavers increasingly began to sign their work, and to expect the recognition previously accorded only to painters. But for many years, carpets and their weavers were not talked about, and in the West at least, their artistry went largely unrecognized.

Happily, things have changed in recent years – not least because the value of fine carpets has been steadily increasing. This investment potential has drawn many new buyers into the field, and once again this has had a knock-on effect on prices as demand has increased. Even so, would-be purchasers should not expect to see immediate profits; rugs should be regarded as medium-term investments, at the very least.

In order to see good returns in the long run, and to enjoy your investment in the interim, it is important to buy the highest quality rugs you can afford. Cheap rugs, like cheap suits, may look good when new, but neither wear well after a few years' use.

Especially if your budget is limited, it is important to remember that the price of a rug, originally at least, is set according to its

Moharamat Qashqa'i, south-west Persia, Fars, wool on cotton, mid-twentieth century, 7'11" × 4'7" (Ref. 1050)
Rugs of this design have traditionally been associated with the Qashqa'i, the most powerful tribal confederation of Fars Province in south-west Persia. The field composition has become known as the *cane moharamat* pattern and is often, as here, embellished with tiny *botehs* or other floral motifs. Such rugs are renowned for their beautiful colour, and this recent example shows that this notable tradition is still alive.

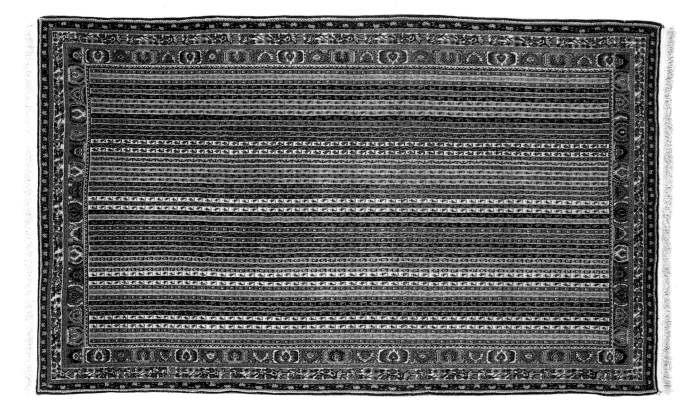

size as well as its quality. Therefore, it makes more sense to buy a very fine small rug than a mediocre large one.

Beyond these basic criteria, it should be recognized that certain types of Persian oriental rugs make better investments than others. Light-toned rugs with large areas of plain colour will tend to become dirty very quickly, and while general grime can be removed quite easily, any heavy staining will mar the beauty of the piece, and thus its value. You will notice as you visit various carpet shops that though the floors may be strewn with rugs, certain cream and pastel pieces are never laid out. Rugs which cannot be put on a shop floor should not be bought as an investment. If they lose value by being walked on in the shop, they will certainly lose value when subjected to the rigours of normal home use.

A good quality carpet which is well cared for will most certainly prove to be a good investment – in addition to being a treasured object of beauty. Consequently, it is most important to have a valuation carried out on your rug for insurance purposes. Since the value of carpets is constantly increasing, it is necessary to have a revaluation every couple of years.

Only if you have a recent insurance valuation certificate will your insurance company honour the policy in cases of theft, fire or water damage. Make sure the valuation is carried out by a reputable dealer. You will have to pay for this service, but the price should be no more than £12–£15. It is a small price to pay for the peace of mind which comes from knowing that one of your most treasured possessions is properly insured.

Medallion, Shirvan, the Caucasus, wool on wool, dated 1330 AH (1911/12 AD), 8'8" × 4'10" (Ref. 1460)

This is a very well-known type of Caucasian village rug from the eastern Shirvan area. Rugs from this region are usually more finely woven than their west Caucasian counterparts and this example is a richly coloured version of this well-known kind. The red motifs at either end of the series of conjoined hexagons in the field are sometimes taken to be the ancient Zoroastrian sun-symbol.

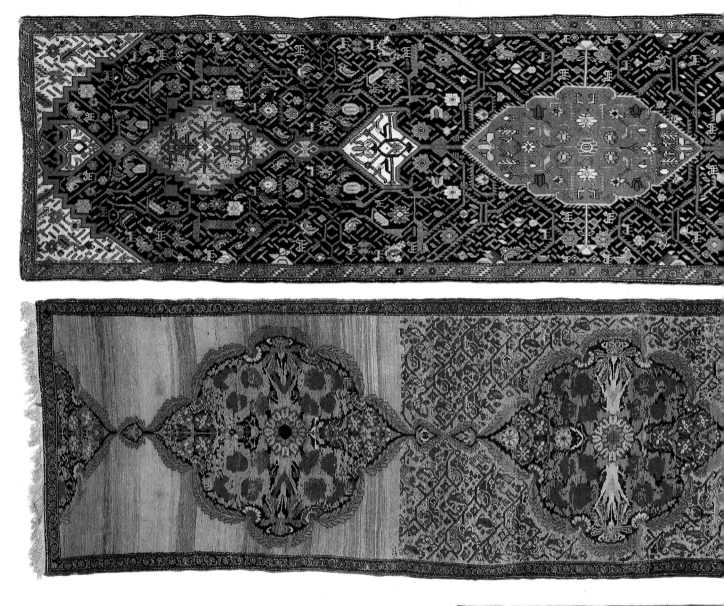

Karabagh, the Caucasus, wool on cotton, early twentieth century, 19'3" × 3'10" (Ref. 874)

This is a good example of the weaving style and palette associated with rugs woven in the Caucasian part of Karabagh, north of the present Soviet border. Certainly there are many affinities with Persian weaving from northern Azerbaijan, but the distinct angularity of drawing suggests a Caucasian origin.

All over gol farangi, Senneh, wool on cotton, dated 1311 AH (1893/4), 14'9" × 3'3" (Ref. 627)

The date on this runner, which appears just above the large *boteh* 'block' to the left of the field, is a little difficult to read but the interpretation we have given is certainly consistent with the design and colour. This is another version of the *gol farangi* with a *boteh* lattice 'block' surrounding the central medallion: a rug almost certainly made for the Western market.

All over design, Bijar, wool on wool, c.1900, 19'0" × 7'3" (Ref. 1116)

A magnificent long rug in particularly bright and vivid colours. The floral design of the field is arranged in three implied vertical rows, while in the border we can see an elegant version of the *gol farangi* pattern.

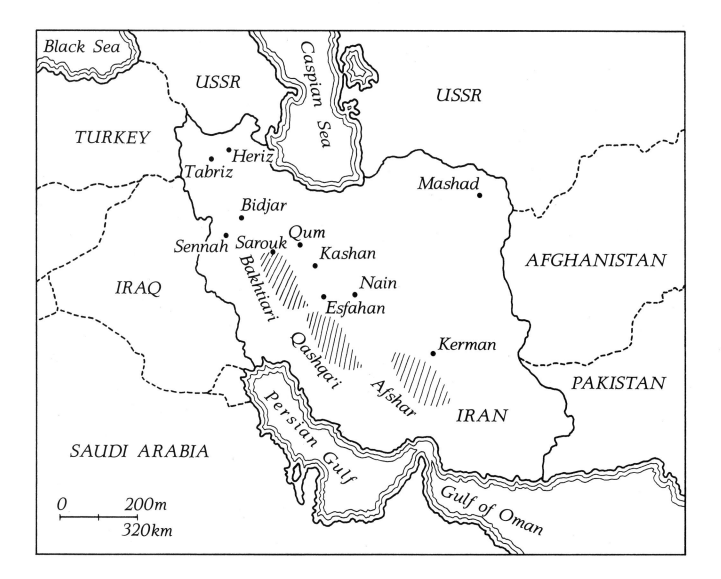

AFSHAR

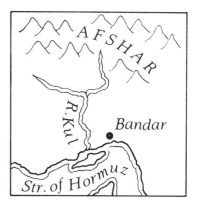

fshar rugs take their name from a nomadic tribe of Turkish origin. Though powerful in the sixteenth century, the tribe was subsequently weakened and divided. Consequently, there are two kinds of Afshar rug. Those from the region of Shiraz tend to be thick, heavy and rather crude in design. Those from the region of Kerman are finer in quality, woven in soft, lustrous wool, and are known as Kerman-Afshars in the trade.

Patterns are mostly geometric. A design of one or two rhombi within an elongated hexagon is common. Motifs of *boteh*, cypresses and the Tree of Life (with straight lines for branches) are also popular. Colours are generally harmonious and subdued.

Warp and weft threads are made of cotton. Rugs are woven with the Turkish knot. Large carpets are rare, with 6' × 4'6" and 5' × 3'6" being the most common sizes.

Boteh all over design, Afshar, south Persia, wool on cotton, early twentieth century, 5'7" × 3'11" (Ref. 547)

The Afshars are one of the great tribal groups of Persia and in the eighteenth century produced the celebrated ruler Nader Shah Afshar, conqueror of Mughal India. They can be found in many parts of the country but the largest and, in terms of weaving, most active group lives to the west of the city of Kerman; it is to this group that this rug should be attributed. Distinctive features of Afshar weaving seen here are the palette, the design in the minor borders and the brocaded end finishes.

BAKHTIARI

Rugs and other weavings associated with the Bakhtiari tribe fall into two groups, the first of which can be described as 'tribal' and the second as 'workshop'. The Bakhtiari, like many of the other great tribal groups of Persia, were formed into a Confederation in 1867 under the leadership of an Ilkhan (supreme *khan* or leader); the particular Bakhtiari sub-tribe from the Ilkhans, the Zarasvand, were already very wealthy by this time, owning large amounts of the Chahar Mahall Valley to the east of the Zagros Mountains and also great areas to the west of the range around the town of Shustar.

The 'tribal' weavings of the Bakhtiari consist not only of large and extremely ornate saddle-bags and other similar woven containers but also superb rugs woven on wool foundations, some of them very large; compared to the workshop rugs, these wool-based pieces are rare. Workshop rugs, although also often of magnificent quality and sometimes huge, can be distinguished from the 'tribal' pieces by the fact that they have cotton foundations. These were made in workshops of various sizes in the hundreds of villages in the Chahar Mahall Valley owned by the Great Khans of the Bakhtiari, as well as in towns in the same region, such as Shar Kord and Shalamzar, which they also owned. In the first part of the twentieth century, when oil was struck on Bakhtiari land and the Great Khans owned a share of Persia's oil revenues, their enormous wealth enabled them to ensure that only the finest materials were used for their rugs. Many such pieces bear inscriptions stating that were woven to the order of a particular *khan*, all of whom built huge mansions and palaces throughout the Chahar Mahall and elsewhere in the late nineteenth and early twentieth centuries.

A number of well-known designs are associated with the Bakhtiari, including the so-called 'garden' or 'garden-tile' pattern of rectangles containing different motifs arranged all over the field, rugs with trees and flowers, and rugs with large central medallions of ornate shape surrounded by flowering branches. Most Bakhtiari rugs, whether tribal or workshop, are dyed entirely with vegetable colours and are among the most splendid and vivid of all nineteenth- and early twentieth-century Persian weavings. The Turkish knot is always used.

Opposite left –

Bakhtiari gol farangi, Chahal Mahall, wool on cotton, first half of the twentieth century, 12'11" × 3'6" (Ref. 1295)
Of all the renderings of the ubiquitous *gol farangi* pattern illustrated in this book, this is perhaps one of the most beautiful, elegant and original. It is interesting to compare this weaving with the Bakhtiari carpet on all wool foundations also illustrated on this page. They have many points in common, particularly the arrangement of motifs, including birds, around the medallions in the field.

Opposite right –

Bakhtiari all over design, Chahar Mahall, wool on wool, second half of the nineteenth century, 16'2" × 6'3" (Ref. 1600)
This is a spectacular rug, the wool-on-wool foundations of which suggest a fairly early date, possibly the 1870s. The extraordinary richness of the colours, all derived from vegetable dyes, is a particular characteristic of the best Bakhtiari weavings. Indeed, most rugs woven in the Chahar Mahall workshops, distinguished by their cotton foundations, were coloured with vegetable dyes well into the twentieth century, a testament to the wealth of the Bakhtiari *khans* and the care and trouble they took with the weavings produced in the factories they owned. The main border has a turreted meander pattern best known, surprisingly, on fifteenth- and sixteenth-century rugs from Ushak in Turkey; it is usually known as the 'Gothic' border.

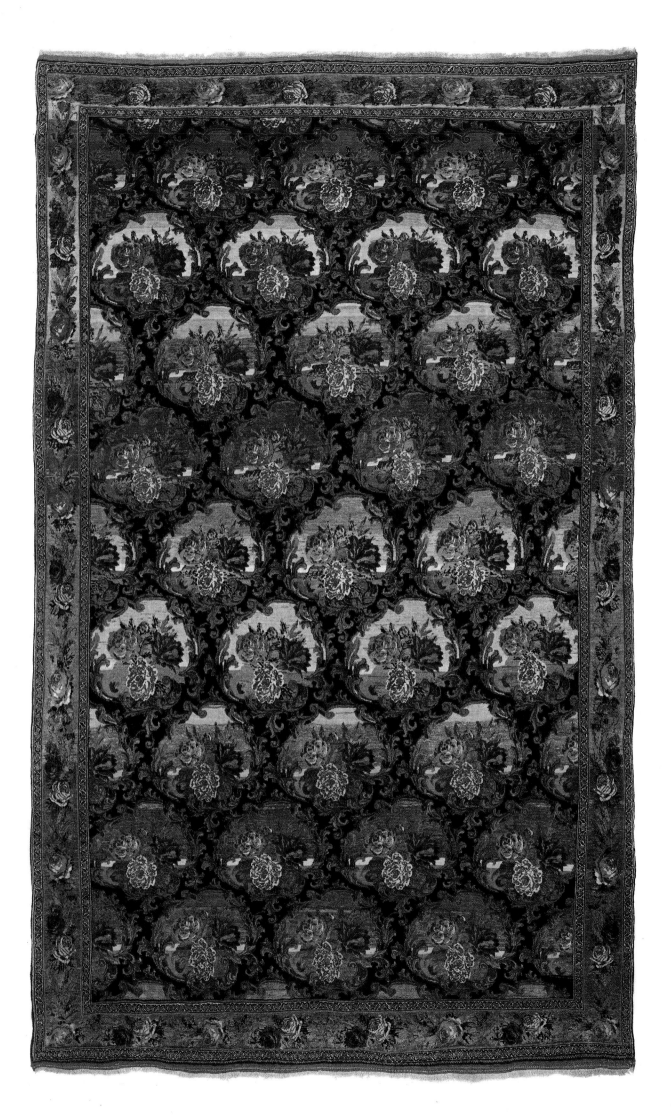

BIJAR

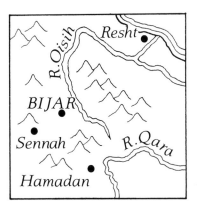

Bijar is a town in the region of Kurdistan. It has had a hard and troubled history. Most recently, it was occupied by the Russians and Turks during World War I. Immediately afterwards it was struck by famine, reducing its population to little more than the size of a small village. Today Bijar has around 10,000 inhabitants, who speak an unusual dialect, part ancient, part modern Persian.

Bijar rugs are highly esteemed for their strength and great weight. The rows of knots are beaten down until extremely compact, giving the impression that there are two layers of weft threads. Because the knots are so firmly packed Bijar rugs should never be folded, since this can strain and even snap the warp threads – instead roll them loosely and carefully, preferably around a reinforcing tube.

Patterns are mainly floral, and despite their robust construction the designs can be extremely delicate. The designs woven in this region are unique, and have never been copied by other tribes. Most common are crowded all-over floral patterns, or medallion designs embellished with *herati* (or fish) motifs. There are also some wonderful carpets with a red 'arabesque' design interwoven with floral ornaments and a well-known group of powerful and splendidly coloured medallion carpets, with a central medallion placed on a wide area of richly-coloured plain field, usually red or blue. Colours tend to be deep and rich, and may include a certain shade of mauve only ever seen in Bidjar rugs.

The *dozar* size (6'6" × 4'3") is most common; other sizes are rarely made. Warp and weft threads are made of wool (sometimes spun from goat hair) or cotton. Rugs are woven with the Turkish knot.

Opposite –

All over gol farangi, Bijar, wool on silk, around 1900, 7'11" × 4'10" (Ref. 1045)
Very few carpets attributed to Bijar have silk foundations and many of those that have are associated with workshops set up in what was then known as the province of Garrus by its governor, Hasan Ali Khan Amir Nizam, in the second half of the nineteenth century; several of these bear inscriptions to this effect. This uninscribed example, bearing one of the most beautiful renderings of the *gol farangi* design we have seen, is exceptionally fine in knotting and is also superbly coloured. One of the masterpieces of Bijar weaving.

All over gol farangi, Karabagh, wool on wool, early twentieth century, 11'0" × 5'3" (Ref. 1543)
A spectacular carpet from the Persian Karabagh. The rich colours and the expansive rendering of the *gol farangi* pattern in the field are most impressive; the main border has an elegantly-drawn floral spiral repeat associated with the more southerly weaving town of Bijar.

ESFAHAN

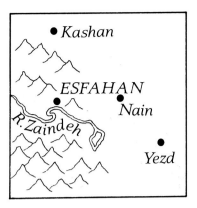

Esfahan is the second largest city in Persia. Its Golden Age was in the seventeenth century, when Shah Abbas the Great made it his capital. During this period, carpets from Esfahan were reputed to be amongst the finest in the world. Of particular renown were the so-called 'Polonaise' carpets woven in the Shah's own factory. These were usually made for presentation to European rulers, and so were of very high quality, often woven in gold and silver thread. Production ended in the eighteenth century when Afghans invaded, and did not recommence until 1910.

The skilled weavers of Esfahan rapidly re-established the city's reputation. They now produce rugs of great delicacy, with finely worked designs and harmonious colours. Symmetrical designs predominate, and birds, the Tree of Life, vases and prayer arches are the most popular patterns. The rose is the emblem of the people of Esfahan. The pile is cut very close to show off intricate designs to their best effect.

The most common sizes are 6'10" × 4'3" and 5'5" × 3'3", although small numbers of very large carpets are woven to commission. These can take many years to complete and are consequently very expensive. Most Esfahan rugs command relatively high prices because of their skilled workmanship. Warp and weft threads are made of silk and cotton. Rugs are woven with the Persian knot.

Opposite –

Shah Abbas all over design, Esfahan, wool on silk, twentieth century, 7'6" × 4'10" (Ref. 1534)
Another splendid and beautifully woven Esfahan. The density of the field drawing, with its 'Shah Abbas' palmettes and *saz* leaves, as well as with its distinctive border design, indicate that this is a comparatively early example of Esfahan 'revivalist' weaving, perhaps from the 1930s.

Moharamat, Esfahan, wool on silk, mid-twentieth century, 7'2" × 5'0" (Ref. 1528)
In its colour and elegant drawing, this lovely carpet is typical of Esfahan weaving during the late Pahlavi period; however, the 'cane' layout of the field (called *moharamat* in Farsi) is quite unusual and is made particularly beautiful by the elegant *boteh* repeat linked by sinuous 'strapwork'.

HERIZ

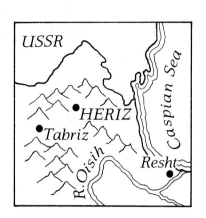

USSR
HERIZ
Tabriz
Caspian Sea
R. Oisih
Resht

Heriz is actually a village in the region of Azerbaijan, though the term covers the rugs of numerous small villages in the area, each distinguished by small differences in design. The most beautiful examples are woven in Heriz itself and in Ahar, Sharabiyan and Kargha.

Heriz rugs are prized for their robustness and resilience. Critics deride their rather coarse knotting, but their charm lies in a characteristic balance of colour and design.

Patterns tend to be markedly geometric, and weavers favour the medallion design. The central motif is usually large, with repeat quarters in the four corners. Colours are generally subtle – predominantly deep red and deep to bright blue – with the corners of the central field picked out in dull ivory. Specific motifs are traditional to individual families.

Before World War I beautiful silk rugs were produced here. These were smooth and thin, and extremely large. Heriz rugs are still some of the largest in Persia.

Smaller sized rugs are rare, but there is seemingly no upper limit – 26′ × 19′6″ and larger are not uncommon. Warp and weft threads are made of cotton. Rugs are woven with the Turkish knot.

Opposite –

Medallion, Heriz, wool on cotton, late nineteenth century, 13′7″ × 11′4″ (Ref. 150)
A typically powerful Heriz medallion carpet with exceptional colour. The relationship between such designs and those found on the rugs from Karabagh and even further north in the province of Azerbaijan remains to be fully explored by scholars. Of particular interest is the design in the main border of this carpet, which derives quite clearly from late seventeenth-century 'vase' carpets attributed to Kerman.

Medallion, Heriz, wool on cotton, early twentieth century, 11′3″ × 8′10″ (Ref. 1605)
Another very typical Heriz medallion rug in characteristic colours and with the spacious design and powerful drawing associated with weavings from this region. Such rugs have been extremely popular in the West for over a hundred years.

KASHAN

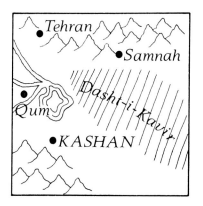

Kashan is an ancient town 160 miles from Tehran with a long history of weaving. The famous 'Ardebil' carpet, now in the Victoria & Albert Museum, was made here. Carpet production actually stopped in the eighteenth century. It was started again in the late nineteenth century by merchants who had the idea of using imported Merino wool for weaving. The practice spread rapidly throughout Persia, though Kashan itself now uses locally produced wool as well. Rugs woven from Merino wool are called Kurk Kashans, and attract higher prices.

Kashan weavers favour classical elongated medallion designs with corner decorations, prayer arches with hanging lamps over monochrome fields and rugs covered with vase motifs, or birds and flowers. Borders are always beautifully patterned and, if inscribed, usually increase the value of a rug. Dyes are of a very high quality, and warm reds and indigo predominate.

Kashan is also famous for its silk brocades, and so it is not surprising to learn that fine silk rugs are woven here too. Whether silk or wool, all Kashans are delicately patterned, with a lustrous, silky pile.

Wool Kashans have cotton warp and weft threads, though silk pile rugs are often woven onto silk. Rugs are woven with the Persian knot.

Opposite –

All over animal design, Kashan, wool on cotton, second half of the nineteenth century, 6'8" × 4'1" (Ref. 1591)
This is a fascinating rug, probably dating from towards the middle of the nineteenth century. Its colour is subdued and the motifs of large cats attacking game are known in almost identical form from Kashan and other carpets woven during the sixteenth and seventeenth centuries. However, the arrangement of these groups and other animals and flowers into a formal pattern repeated in mirror image from top to bottom, with a central divide, is very unusual and has a most archaic flavour.

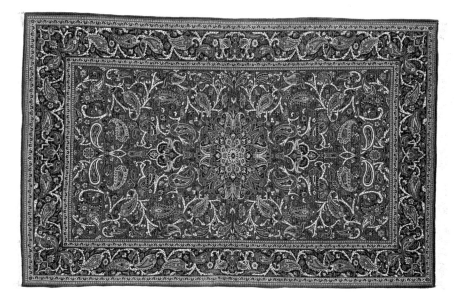

Boteh medallion, Kashan, wool on cotton, early twentieth century, 6'9" × 4'4" (Ref. 1538)
The predominant red-blue palette is what we would expect of a Kashan rug from the early twentieth century. However, the extraordinary range of pale blues, vivid greens, pinks and other colours within the field is also something one associates with the best Kashan weaving. The design of this rug, with its elegant but quietly stated central medallion, is based on a beautifully drawn version of the *boteh* motif.

KERMAN

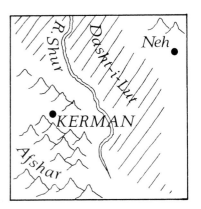

Kerman rugs come from the city of that name and the surrounding area in central south-east Iran. The people of Kerman are widely renowned for their great artistic skill, which is perhaps a reaction to the desolate landscape of that region.

In this barren desert landscape no flowers will grow, and so the weavers cover their carpets with beautiful and intricate floral patterns in a wide variety of designs. The medallion design is popular, its intricate patterns often highlighted by the use of a plain-coloured (open) ground. In other rugs the ground is densely packed with floral motifs, with or without a medallion. The borders are often decorated with patterns similar to those used in the main body of the carpet.

'Laver Kerman' is the name given to particularly fine examples of old rugs from this region. The word Laver is actually a corruption of Ravar, the name of a particular village in this region renowned for its weaving. In all types of Kerman the warp and weft threads are usually of cotton with a wool pile. The rugs are generally quite fine with average knots counts of 190 or more.

Opposite –

All over design, Kerman, wool on cotto.., late nineteenth – early twentieth century, 21'10″ × 14'1″ (Ref. 1569)
Both in colour and design an unusual and rather splendid old Kerman carpet with fine silk (*kurk*) wool, which seems to owe much to contemporaneous Kashan weaving. It is interesting to note the skill with which the multiplicity of floral and cloud-band motifs in the field are organized into implied medallions; the colour of the piece is also exceptionally fine.

Medallion design, Kerman, wool on cotton, early twentieth century, 18'2″ × 9'5″ (Ref. 1016)
In the nineteenth century, the central Persian city of Kerman was a producer of exotic and expensive shawls woven for the market in Europe, due in part to cheap local production. The ubiquitous *boteh* design is still widely known as the Paisley Pattern after the Scottish shawl-weaving town which took up the production of shawls in the nineteenth century. Many Kermani shawl-weavers also turned their hands to carpet making. The result was a distinctive Kerman style in which the usual format of field surrounded by borders gave way to a mixture of shawl and carpet styles. ·

MASHAD

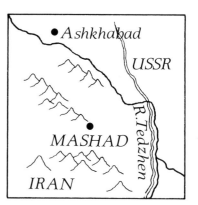

ashad, meaning Place of Martyrdom, is the capital of Khorasan and one of the most important holy cities of Persia.

Mashad has a long history of weaving, but at the beginning of this century dealers from nearby Tabriz established a number of factories in the city and brought in weavers to work there. The new factory workers preferred the Turkish knot, while locals continued to use the Persian. As a result Mashad rugs are peculiar in that they may be made with either knot. The city's most famous factory, the Emogli factory, was at its height in the 1930s. It was renowned for the delicate beauty and harmonious colouring of its rugs.

At the turn of the century well-proportioned central medallion designs were very popular, and were valued for their elegant curves and intricate arabesques. Current designs include closely-packed floral patterns and, occasionally, animal motifs. Colours are characteristically dark, with deep blue and red grounds predominating. Mashad borders are usually richly patterned.

The city is also known for its so-called Chuval rugs in which the pattern runs widthwise, rather than lengthwise as is usual. Originally these pieces were made into bags. Traditionally they were woven as 'test pieces' by young girls of marriageable age, and consequently there are many fine examples of this type.

Mashad rugs are recognizable by their sloping knots, whether Turkish or Persian, and tend to have a deep, soft pile. Warp and weft threads are of cotton. Rugs are available in a wide range of sizes, though generally the larger ones are the most attractive.

Opposite –

Medallion, Mashad, wool on cotton, mid-twentieth century, signed: Saber, 23'0" × 16'5" (Ref. 1579)

Saber was one of the best-known post-war *ustad* in Mashad, the capital of the easternmost Persian province of Khorasan and its main weaving centre. The signature of the workshop appears in the centre of the topmost white ground guard border. The field design is an adaptation of the sixteenth-century Ardebil carpets, one of which is in the Victoria and Albert Museum, London and the other in the Los Angeles County Museum. Despite the variations which have been played on the original, both in design and colour, the central medallion and corners surrounded by lobed palmettes and the pendant lamps at top and bottom of the medallion have all been retained.

All over boteh design, Doroksh, wool on cotton, late nineteenth century, 7'11" × 5'2" (Ref. 737)

In contrast to some of the plain field and medallion Doroksh carpets illustrated in this book, this example shows the tight all-over patterning associated with many Khorasan weaving centres in the late nineteenth and early twentieth centuries and which reached its apogee in the work of the master weaver Emoghli of Mashad in the first half of the twentieth century. The colour of this rug is particularly noteworthy and gives softness to the regularity of the packed *boteh* repeat. The overall design itself is clearly derived from early nineteenth-century shawls. This is a very finely woven example of its kind.

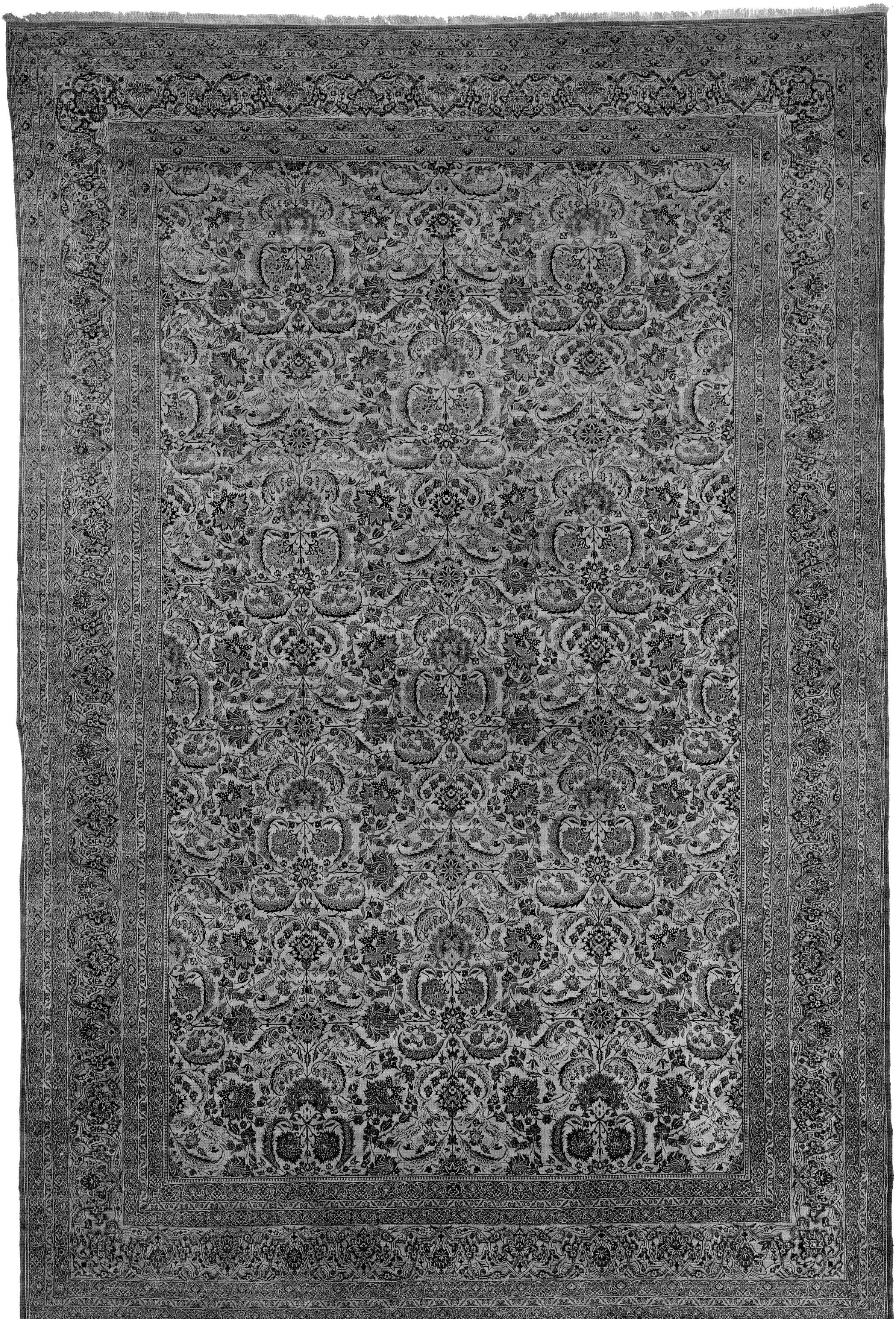

NAIN

Nain is a town of approximately 10,000 inhabitants, not far from Esfahan. Its carpet industry was established shortly before World War II; prior to this the town produced traditional garments called *abas*. This industry was destroyed by the fashion for Western-style clothing, and the craftsmen turned their skills to carpet weaving instead. Already used to working with fine yarns, the weavers made delicate rugs right from the start, and their fame spread rapidly. Nain still produces the most finely-knotted rugs, with counts usually starting at around 400 knots per square inch, and sometimes exceeding an amazing 645 knots per square inch.

Such finely-knotted rugs are very labour intensive, and consequently production is slow. Demand consistently outstrips supply so prices are high, though still representing good value for money.

As a recent carpet-producing centre, the town has no traditional patterns to draw on, concentrating instead on classical designs. The medallion design is particularly popular, and the ground is always intricately patterned with close-packed motifs. Backgrounds are usually light, overlayed with conservative colours. The dyes used are always of the highest quality.

Warp and weft threads are of cotton. Rugs are woven using the Persian knot. The pile is usually very close-trimmed to show off the intricate design.

Opposite –

All over design, Nain, wool on cotton, twentieth century, 12'5" × 8'5" (Ref. 844) Both in design and colour, this is quite unusual for a Nain rug, especially if we compare it to the other characteristic examples we have illustrated. The ground is in an attractive pale yellow and many colours have been employed for the delicate floral repeat in the field.

Medallion, Nain, wool and silk on cotton, twentieth century, 18'11" × 12'10" (Ref. 1490)
The restrained colouring of Nain carpets has made them very popular in the West. One should note, however, that even on so large a scale as this, the drawing of the individual floral motifs, including 'Shah Abbas' palmettes and curling *saz* leaves, the design retains its delicate fluidity.

QASHQA'I

The Qashqa'i are a tribal people from the Fars region. In Persia they have a reputation as the most powerful tribe, with the best horsemen and weavers. Although most of the nomads have now settled, they continue to use traditional horizontal looms, spin wool from their own sheep and blend dyes according to ancient plant recipes.

Qashqa'i rugs tend to be rather loosely knotted, and hence not as hard-wearing as they might be. They are, however, rich in detail, with many unique patterns improvized from traditional family motifs. Popular images include naïve interpretations of animals, birds, horsemen and trees, and the classic *boteh* motif. The three-trunked tree of life is a common design. Borders are imaginative and varied, and striped bands at either end are common. The Qashqa'i people have a great love of colour which is very evident in their rugs, which are bright but never clashing. A certain subdued rusty red colour is particularly highly prized.

The Qashqa'i also weave beautiful bags and horse blankets. These blankets, known as *juleh asp*, have long tassles round the edges to keep flies at bay, and make wonderful wall decorations.

Qashqa'i rugs are usually made of particularly soft and lustrous wool. Warp and weft threads are also of wool, the warp sometimes made of dark goat hair. Most common sizes are 6' × 4' and 5' × 3'3".

Opposite –

Medallion animal design, Qashqa'i, south-west Persia, Fars, wool on wool, second half of the nineteenth century, 8'4" × 4'1" (Ref. 1541)
This is an outstanding antique Qashqa'i tribal rug in remarkably good condition for its age and is particularly interesting for having an ivory ground, an unusual feature among the several known rugs of this well-known design group. The large number of stylized animals and birds, as well as the diagonal comb-like motifs, are characteristic features. The rows of squares seen at the extremities are taken as almost certain indications of either a Qashqa'i or Luri (another major tribe) origin. A rug of considerable importance and rarity.

Boteh Qashqa'i, south-west Persia, Fars, wool on wool, signed and dated 1322 AH (1905/6 AD), 6'1" × 4'5" (Ref. 1548)
Another delightful *boteh* rug of the type associated with the Kashkuli tribe of the Qashqa'i Confederation. The filigree-like drawing of the field is particularly noteworthy and this example has a quite unusual and attractive floral meander pattern on the ivory ground of the main border.

QUM

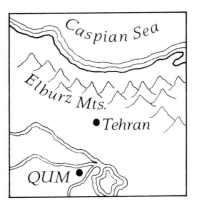

Qum is an ancient town in the Tehran region. Its carpet industry, however, was not established until the 1930s, when looms were set up within the town itself, not in neighbouring villages as is more usual in Iran.

As a comparatively new weaving centre, the town has no traditional designs of its own, but borrows instead from neighbouring regions – in particular Senneh, Kashan and Esfahan. This is not to say that Qum rugs are without originality. They combine design elements from various traditions, maybe the border of one with the field of another, to create unique patterns.

The most popular patterns are the classic garden design; striped rugs in which lines of colour and ornament run the length of the carpet; illustrative carpets depicting birds, animals and hunting scenes (details usually picked out in silk), and prayer rugs. Most rugs have an ivory background, often combined with pink and a particular shade of light green which is extremely rare in other Persian oriental carpets.

Qum rugs are not as delicate as those from Kashan or Esfahan, but are still amongst the finest in Iran. In the last forty years the town has begun to produce part silk and pure silk rugs which have enhanced yet further their reputation amongst buyers. Warp threads are sometimes silk, and in some rare carpets the weft threads are silk as well. Rugs are also woven in silk and wool on a wool warp and cotton weft. Rugs are woven using the Persian knot. Sizes range from 6'10" × 4'3" up to 9'9" × 13".

Opposite –

Tree of Life, Qum, silk on silk, twentieth century, signed: Piromand, 6'9" × 4'7" (Ref. 1405)
Rugs from the holy city of Qum do not, apparently, pre-date the twentieth century; certainly none of the surviving Safavid carpets have been attributed to it. In the modern era, Qum has become renowned for its silk rugs and one of the best-known designs is a single large lily, elegantly and sinuously drawn as here and surrounded by floral sprays. The palette of this rug, however, especially its dark blue ground, is a little unusual.

Landscape design, Qum, silk on silk, twentieth century, signed: Qum–Asgarie, 5'0" × 3'5" (Ref. 1034)
A landscape-shaped rug with a landscape design, in which the warps run at right-angles to the long side. Pure silk Qums are among the most highly regarded Persian weavings of the last fifty years and this example is by one of the best known *ustads* of the city, which is a few miles north of Kashan. The pale blue of the rocky pool is a particularly pleasing feature, as is the succession of leading and running animals and birds in the main border.

SAROUK

arouk is a village in the Arak region in the north-west of Iran. The area is known for its agricultural activity as well as its weaving.

Weavers favour the classic medallion design, and these rugs are often beautifully ornamented with arabesque designs which are attractively angular in appearance. Borders, in comparison, are usually quite simple. A particular shade of coral pinkish-red is typical of rugs from this area which is combined with more subdued shades of ivory, dark blue and green.

Examples made before about 1915 tend to have a very close-cropped pile and compact knotting. Later examples usually have longer pile intended to appeal to the export market, in particular America. Warp and weft thread are typically of cotton. The rugs are woven using the Persian knot.

Opposite –

Flowered design, Sarouk, wool on cotton, twentieth century, 13'7" × 10'4" (Ref. 137)
Looking at the finest late nineteenth and early twentieth-century Persian carpets, one is struck by the large number representing a direct design continuum with the Golden Age of Safavid weaving during the sixteenth and seventeenth centuries. This example is no exception, the beautifully coloured field of interlocking panels reminding one immediately of seventeenth-century Kerman carpets.

Mahal, wool on cotton, mid-twentieth century, 14'0" × 11'0" (Ref. 1577)
In both design and colour, this represents one of the best known types of late nineteenth – early twentieth century north-west Persian weaving. Vast numbers of such rugs were made in Sarouk, Mahal, Lilihan, Sultanabad (Arak) and elsewhere for export to the West, where their rose-coloured grounds were extremely fashionable. At their best, they are very beautiful, especially those woven with particularly silky wool.

SENNEH

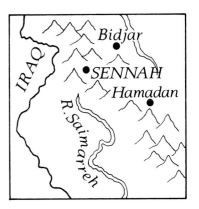

enneh is in Iranian Kurdistan. It is often erroneously said by writers that this is the old name for Sanandaj, the beautiful capital of the province, but this does not seem to be true. Senneh, like Ravar near Kerman, was a small village which produced some fine weavings and which gave its name to all the rugs from both its own looms and from Sanandaj. Rugs are fine and thin, very different from other types of rug made in Kurdistan.

Traditional designs have varied little for centuries. Patterns are intricate and finely worked, covering the entire ground of the rug to give a mosaic-like effect. Delicate floral patterns predominate. The weavers' passion for intricate pattern is so great that examples of medallion carpets with plain grounds are extremely rare. Colours are mainly vegetable-based, and are combined with fine artistic judgement, so that it is hard to say what colour, if any, predominates in a rug. Grounds tend to be ivory or blue, sprinkled with touches of sometimes vivid colour, yet the overall effect is wonderfully harmonious. Borders, in contrast, are usually narrow and simple.

Senneh also produces some of the most beautiful *kilims* in Iran. These are woven with the same exquisite taste, and frequently include the same designs, as are used in knotted rugs. Their weave tends to be firmer than is usual in *kilim* production.

The rugs are woven in very high quality wool, usually taken from young sheep. They are woven with the Turkish knot (though paradoxically the 'Senneh' is an alternative name for the Persian knot). Most common sizes are 6'6" × 4'3" and 5' × 3'3" – generally, larger carpets are quite old. Very fine examples are rare.

Opposite –

All over design, Senneh, kilim, wool on cotton, early twentieth century, 6'7" × 4'3" (Ref. 1623)
This is a typically finely woven *kilim* from Senneh, with a very elegant version of the *herati* pattern. The colours are also typical of Senneh *kilims* of this period. A very fine and most attractive sample.

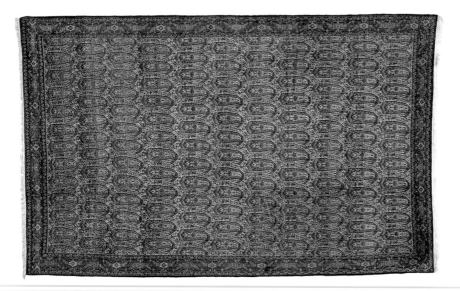

Senneh, wool on cotton, mid-twentieth century, 13'10" × 8'7" (Ref. 1048)
Rugs, both pile and flat-woven, with all-over *boteh* repeat patterns, have been woven in Senneh since the late eighteenth century. This example is typical of a specific group which have *botehs* drawn in this particular way, with these colours and on an ivory ground.

TABRIZ

Tabriz is the capital of Azerbaijan, in north-west Persia. Since the seventeenth century it has been one of the foremost carpet-producing towns in the country. Even today its weavers are reputedly among the most skilled, and work with great speed using a special knotting hook.

Tabriz weavers favour the central medallion design with repeat corner decorations, thought to be inspired by hand-tooled book covers. These rugs are richly ornamented with elegant arabesques and intertwining flowers across the entire field. Backgrounds are usually red, blue or ivory, patterned with a variety of subtle shades. Tabriz is also famous for its pictorial rugs. The four seasons design is popular, as are pictures of mosques and palaces. However, the most frequent designs portray Persia's four greatest poets – Firdausi, Hafiz, Saadi and Omar Khayam.

Tabriz rugs are extremely hard-wearing. Warp and weft threads are of cotton. Rugs are woven with either the Persian or Turkish knot, although more usually the latter. Tabriz has exported rugs for many years, and as a result they are produced in a great range of sizes and shapes.

Opposite –

All over design, Tabriz, wool and cotton, mid-twentieth century, Signed: Taghi Pur, 21'0" × 14'9" (Ref. 1364)
This carpet, bearing the signature of an *ustad* in a tiny cartouche, has a field design closely based on seventeenth-century 'vase' carpets from Kerman in central Persia.

Medallion, Tabriz, wool and silk on silk, twentieth century, signed: Benaham, 5'3" × 3'4" (Ref. 1447)
Another spectacular Tabriz weaving of the highest quality. The medallion, pendant and corners composition of this rug recall the wonderful Tabriz medallion carpets of the early sixteenth century.

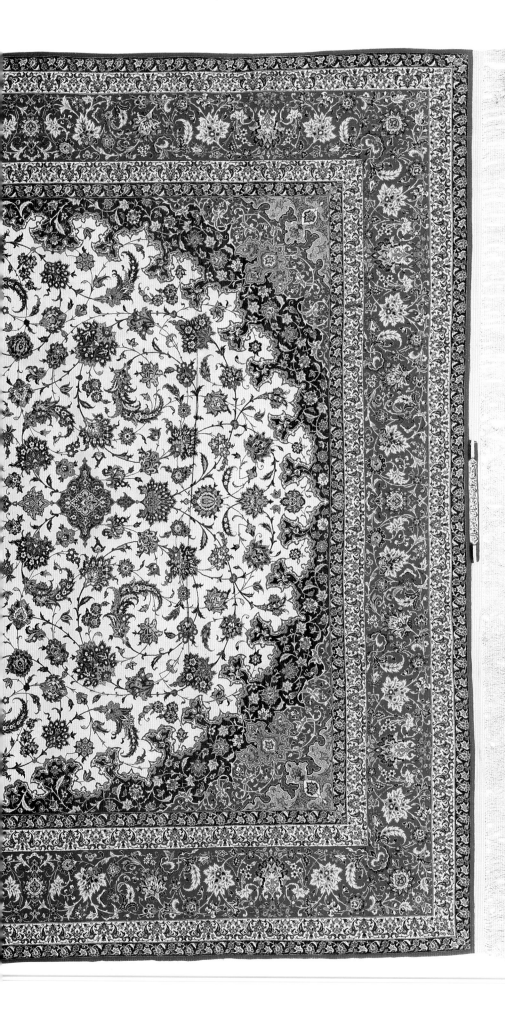

Medallion, Esfahan, wool and silk on silk, mid-twentieth century, signed: Iran–Esfahan–Sadghe–Sirafian, 14'10" × 10'2" (Ref. 1564)

This represents late Pahlavi Esfahan weaving at its most luxurious and in both design and colour is an archetypal example. Sirafian was certainly the most famous and highly regarded *ustad* in Iran in the post-war decades and this carpet is of exceptional quality. It was woven under the direction of one of the second generation members of the family. The style of this carpet was not confined to any particular workshop, but is associated above all with Esfahan and with Sirafian; it was copied in many other weaving centres, especially Nain. Around the central sixteen-lobed 'star' medallion, swirling 'Shah Abbas' palmettes and delicately curling *saz* leaves are arranged in a delightful arabesque. All genuine 'sirafians' are very finely woven but it is unusual to find a carpet of this size so finely knotted.

Overleaf –

Medallion mosque design, Tabriz, silk and wool on cotton, twentieth century, 15'1" × 11'6" (Ref. 156)

A particular group of Persian carpets associated with the Pahlavi period take as their inspiration the painted or tiled interior of mosque domes. Such carpets are not associated with any one workshop or city but the greatest examples always seem to be either from Tabriz or Esfahan. Because of the association with mosques, such carpets – and this is an excellent example – have a greater, more spiritual, dimension beyond the merely decorative, a dimension often lost on the Western viewer.